The Compassionate Life

Coach yourself into a
fully **engaged** and **influential** life

Communities of Trust - Jerry Goebel

Jerry Goebel, MBA, D.Min.

Communities of Trust - Jerry Goebel

goebeljerry@me.com

www.communitiesoftrust-jerrygoebel.com

Trusting Communities ~ Engaged People

Table of Contents

I
Compassion

The Three Fires of Compassion

Compassion has three primary components:

1. *Passion:* A fire in your belly
2. *Purpose:* A unifying force in your life
3. *People:* A uniting force in the lives of those you encounter

1. PASSION: A FIRE IN YOUR BELLY

Compassion; it springs from a purpose or cause that inspires you, that makes you want to take action on a deep, personal level. We might even say it puts a fire in your belly.

Consider someone who has inspired you — either personally or historically. For example, the Rev. Dr. Martin Luther King, Jr., driven by his strong desire for social equality, Dr. King spent the latter part of his life leading marches and organizing events that brought to light many of the inequalities of his day. People remember him most for a 17-minute speech he gave on the steps of the Lincoln Memorial on August 28, 1963. In that speech, Dr. King made the following statement:

> "I have a dream that one day this nation will rise up and live out the true meaning of its creed: "We hold these truths to be self-evident, that all men are created equal.

> "I have a dream that one day on the red hills of Georgia the sons of former slaves and the sons of former slave

owners will be able to sit down together at the table of brotherhood.

"I have a dream that one day even the state of Mississippi, a state sweltering with the heat of injustice, sweltering with the heat of oppression, will be transformed into an oasis of freedom and justice.

"I have a dream that my four little children will one day live in a nation where they will not be judged by the color of their skin but by the content of their character.

"I have a dream today."

The Rev. Dr. King's life was extinguished at the Lorraine Hotel in Memphis, Tennessee on April 4th, 1968. He was only 39. However a sniper's bullet could not extinguish his light. The fire of his compassion ignited a generation and continues today.

Compassionate people are on fire with a purpose, they aren't cool — they're hot. The fire burning inside of them can't help but catch others alight as well. As you consider what moves you, consider also who inspires you. What ignites a fire in your belly?

People often say, "You can't help others until you have your own act together."

Nothing could be further from the truth. When you examine the world's greatest influencers, like the Rev. Dr. Martin Luther King Jr., their inner resolve deepened as they offered assistance to others. A better way to view inner confidence is this, "Sometimes you just have to fake it 'til you feel it."

In truth, we receive more when give. It is similar to how balanced adults view holidays over time. When we were children our joy was in receiving gifts, as we mature, we find the true joy in giving.

Nothing undermines self-esteem more rapidly than focusing solely on personal wants without the perspective of gratitude or service. This viewpoint only serves to reduce our influence in the world and our self-confidence. It seems inverted, but the more we focus on our own wants, the less joy we experience and the smaller our sphere of influence.

> **The more we focus on our own wants, the less joy we experience and the smaller our sphere of influence.**

Developing this list will give you something to always return to when you are feeling self-focused or perhaps we might even call it, "meo-centric."

Find video clips, quotes, pictures or songs that move you and start developing a file that will inspire and help you keep perspective when you detect you're becoming meo-centric.

(See Exercise 1.1 at the back of this chapter)

2. A PURPOSE A UNIFYING FORCE IN YOUR LIFE

The second component of compassion is a force unifying your personal life and propelling you in a focused direction.

As soon as you state a purpose — and especially if you commit it to paper — your mind starts working consciously and subconsciously towards that reality. It compels you personally, spiritually, physically, financially and even in your relationships — attracting people who will support your cause.

When you have a unifying purpose, it helps you stand against the temptations to give in or give up on your beliefs. It will especially help you stand against the greatest temptations, 1) to succumb to a life of ease, 2) to live solely for attention or approval and 3) to use the power of manipulation to meet your needs regardless of its impact on others.

Rosa Parks, another pioneer of civil rights, once framed the importance of having a purpose with these words, "Stand for something or you will fall for anything. Today's mighty oak is yesterday's nut that held its ground."

Even while you're sleeping your subconscious mind works towards your purpose. Most of our creative ideas happen when we've digested information and then stopped concentrating on that material. Neuroscientists call this "Transient Hypofrontality." A lengthy phrase meaning we have to interrupt intentional thought so the brain can play with information. Transient means temporary and hypofrontality means to reduce the powerful force of the human frontal lobe. This allows your thoughts to "meander" to multiple areas of the brain which is fundamental to creativity.

When we normally process information, the frontal lobe is like a person who says, "I need to go to the store and get milk." He jumps into his car, drives to the store and back home without ever noticing the scenery around him.

Transient Hypofrontality is similar to a person who instead says, "I'm going for a walk and will pick up a carton of milk while I'm out."

That person wanders, taking time to admire the scenery and enjoy the stroll. All of the time his brain is unconsciously processing the material previously consumed and creating new and creative applications for that material.

Much of our experience in education focused on the memorization and recitation aspect of the learning process, not on the creative aspect (transient hypofrontality). There is little time allotted for creativity and application in our education system and whatever has been memorized is lost after the recitation piece (testing). This is actually an advanced function of the human brain called "synapse pruning (pruning information that isn't critical to long-term survival)."

Everything the brain doesn't seem to habitually need or use creatively is pruned.

If we didn't prune information our behavioral responses would become cumbersome and slow, unable to process information rapidly. These immediate responses were pretty important when the human species had only a few decisions needed for survival, "Do I run or be eaten by this saber-toothed tiger?"

Information that is habitually required becomes integrated processes of immediate responses called, "Cognitive Pathways."

"See the danger, respond, think about it later."

Everything the brain doesn't seem to habitually need or use creatively is pruned. Which is why, as soon as a teacher says, "This is going to be on the test," the brain identifies the material as temporary and rejects it after the test is complete.

Ergo, once fear or stress is introduced into the learning process, we might as well be teaching a chair because we're not teaching the student in it.

It is why so many of us sat in classrooms for years learning, math, science, history or foreign languages only to forget all of the information shortly after the test was complete.

To be creative, we must allow the frontal lobe to relax and let the information we gather flow to multiple centers of the brain. It is one of the primary reasons recess, art and music may be the most important periods of a child's day and our hobbies may be the most important activities in an adult's life.

I encourage educators; "We need to teach all of our classes before recess, lunch or a music or art period. We need to build in transient hypofrontality into our classes or we're simply wasting our students time — and future."

Next time you — or the people you are leading — are learning new and important information, build in your own time for transient hypofrontality. If you want to build deeper attachments to the purpose in your life you also have to make time for play (transient hypofrontality).

> **If you want to build deeper attachments to the purpose in your life you also have to make time for play (transient hypofrontality).**

How can you play with your purpose?

Play can be through games, meditation, exercise, the arts or a conversation. We'll discuss more about the importance of play later in Chapter III.

To be better at innovation, we must become better at playing. Similarly to deepen our purpose, we need to allow for transient hypofrontality. Essentially, we must play with our purpose to make it real.

3. PEOPLE: A UNITING FORCE IN THE LIVES OF THOSE YOU ENCOUNTER

Finally, compassion not only unifies your own drive towards a *compelling purpose,* it also helps you to motivate and unite others towards a *hopeful destination.*

Your ability to influence the world around you is directly tied to your ability to motivate others to pursue a common purpose. Influential people can articulate a captivating vision and unite a community of people around it. It is the most powerful force in humankind. Margaret Mead, famed anthropologist and author, stated; "Never doubt that a small group of thoughtful, committed, citizens can change the world. Indeed, it is the only thing that ever has."

Everyone has influence — positive or negative. Even our indifference influences, when we shun involvement in the issues around us we are giving power to those who would victimize others.

Holocaust survivor and Noble Prize winner, Elie Wiesel, once stated, "The opposite of love is not hate, it's indifference. The opposite of art is not ugliness, it's indifference. The opposite of faith is not heresy, it's indifference. And the opposite of life is not death, it's indifference."

Some people use their influence in a negative way. That's not unusual in times or situations where people think cynicism is wisdom and sarcasm is humor. However, these two tools (cynicism and sarcasm) immobilize people — they don't mobilize us to act for the betterment of others or ourselves.

Most people who are immobilized focus on what they *can't do* and *don't have*. In contrast, people with a positive influence focus on what they can do — no matter how small — and on what they *do have* — no matter how little. Influential people don't focus on the size of the problem they focus on the depth of their commitment.

Influential people don't focus on the size of the problem they focus on the depth of their commitment.

This is one thing I had to continually address when I was more active as a chaplain in detention centers, jails and prisons. The system is often skewed with a focus that emphasizes what the person has done wrong in the past rather than what could be done better in the future.

Please don't misunderstand me, it is important to look back at our mistakes — especially the ones done intentionally that have hurt others. We can't ask or receive forgiveness if we don't understand the deprivation our action may have caused others — and by doing so also harmed ourselves.

However it is just as important to focus on retraining our cognitions and behaviors to avoid those errors in the future.

One reoccurring problem I encountered was the questions people would ask themselves when they focused upon the errors of the past. It seems obvious that if we ask the wrong questions, we'll get the wrong answers. For example, perhaps a person does poorly at a task and asks, "Why am I so stupid?"

The only possible responses to that question are negative. For example, "I'm stupid because..."

Instead, we need to do a "Question-ectomy." Cut out the negative questions in your life and replace them with positive ones. For example, "What can I do to improve my behavior next time?"

Question-ectomies are something we need to practice multiple times until they become habits. Think about circumstances in your life where you could have enhanced your behavior or the results of an endeavor then create a strategy for responding with positive questions.

See Exercise 1.4 to develop your own Question-Ectomies.

Instead of focusing on errors, sports psychologists often have client's think about the last time they performed optimally. Then, they have the athlete visualize mastering the behavior perfectly in multiple scenarios.

For example, if a professional tennis player hit a wayward shot, instead of stomping around and throwing the racket while focusing on what went wrong, the coach would have the player mindfully take a break and visualize the last time he or she hit the same shot perfectly.

The brain cannot differentiate between the actual tennis shot and a detailed visualization of it.

This theory doesn't just apply to sports; you can apply it to varied behaviors you wish to improve in multiple facets of your life. We can create new and positive cognitive pathways by visualizing stories about healthy outcomes. The more we tell a story — and the more detail we use — the more our minds believe the story. This can be negative or beneficial if you recognize the power of positive story-telling in your life.

What are the components of positive story-telling?

1. Recreate a positive outcome

2. Visualize the event in detail

3. Imagine the feelings associated with the outcome (perhaps initial confusion or stress followed by determination and then elation)

4. Use as many senses in re-telling (or writing) the story as positive (imagine not just the sights, but also tastes, sounds and smells if possible).

As you grow the positive in your life, people will be attracted to your attitude and effectiveness — and no one can argue with compassionate effectiveness. The key to growing influence is to master one, vital action and let your effectiveness speak for itself. No marketing strategy in the world can match the power of effectiveness and word-of-mouth.

I experienced this in our detention-based outreaches in Washington State. While I was on an extended mission trip, experienced volunteers recruited and trained a new group of mentors for our program, "Significant Conversations."

Adults in this program would share conversations with young people that our trained leaders facilitated.

Upon returning, I encountered a new volunteer to our program in a way that was quite intriguing. I met her in the lobby of the detention center, her name was Shirley and her guide dog's name was Sam. That's right, she was blind and well into her seventies and yet she spent an hour a week mentoring incarcerated young people.

She did not know who I was, so I took the opportunity to ask her about the program and how she enjoyed it. She told me it was the most exhilarating hour of her week and was changing her life as well as the lives of those whom she mentored.

Then, Shirley proceeded to recruit me!

She said, "You listen well, you should be a part of this program!"

A blind, 70-plus year old woman was recruiting me to a program I had started!

I realized immediately that one Shirley, turned loose in a community, was better than a thousand or even ten thousand fliers.

Be effective, be consistent, be positive and people will gather around your compassionate focus.

THE FIVE PERCENT TRICK

Another helpful idea is the "Five Percent Principle." If a task seems overwhelming to you, ask yourself, "What can I do to become Five Percent more effective in this area of my life?"

Examples:

- If I were to increase my knowledge of nutrition by five percent...
- If I were to better my relationship with my child by five percent...
- If I were to be five percent more active this week...

Instead of thinking how to improve your whole life immediately, how would you improve it incrementally by five percent a day or week?

I used this concept at work camps where young people came from across the nation to restore houses for those who were elderly and/or had few resources. When groups arrived, they would often look at the project as a whole and you could see the disappointment on their faces. "We will never get this work done."

However, we would begin by taking one small task at a time, "Let's just focus on fixing the front porch right now."

When we had completed that task, it gave people the confidence — and enthusiasm — to move on to the next task. Soon the whole project was complete and people were overjoyed and amazed at all they'd accomplished working together in such a short period of time.

So ask yourself, "What is the five percent solution you could focus on this week that would have the greatest mobilizing impact on your life?"

"What is the five percent solution you could focus on this week that would have the greatest mobilizing impact on your life?"

SOCIAL QUESTION-ECTOMIES

Not only is this principal of asking the right question (Question-ectomies and Five Percent growth) applicable to personal areas in our lives, it can also be applied to larger possibilities for growth in your community or our world. Issues like poverty or prejudice can seem unconquerable when viewed through the incorrect lens. Yet, if we, 1) apply the five percent principal, and 2) challenge the definition of the premise behind these issues (question-ectomies), it will affect how we respond to them.

Look at the following re-definitions of social issues and consider how redefining them would help people deal with them in a whole new way.

Prejudice

- Definition 1: Prejudice is a deeply embedded belief of hatred towards others of a certain class, race, gender, sexual orientation or religion, or
- Definition 2: Prejudice cannot withstand relationship

Rather than trying to convince people to think differently, I can create common causes between people of different backgrounds. For example, in one community where I lived, people were divided by deeply held racial misconceptions. This is the heart of prejudice — "pre-judging" people we've never even met.

Yet, children from both groups played in the same park and that became our common cause.

In the process of working together to clean the park, people brought food and started conversations. In some cases, where people could not communicate due to language barriers, they still grew mutual respect by working side-by-side to get the job done.

Build relationships — destroy prejudice.

Poverty

- Definition 1: A lack of resources, or
- Definition 2: A lack of healthy relationships

When I see poverty as a relationship issue and not just a resource issue, I can focus on building a network of skilled and caring people around those who are impoverished rather than a solitary strategy of redistributing resources.

Build relationships — destroy poverty.

Wealth

- Definition 1: The accumulation of financial assets, or
- Definition 2: The ability to give

If a person makes millions of dollars a year but will not give anything more than they are forced to because of taxes — they don't consider themselves wealthy enough.

Alternatively, if a person only has a bowl of rice and shares it with a hungry neighbor, they consider themselves able to give.

Herein are the differences between a successful and a meaningful life. Success is what I make for myself; meaning is what I give to others.

The two are not mutually exclusive. Many successful people use their resources in a meaningful way, alleviating poverty or prejudice in the world. They just view the "goal" of their wealth as more than the *accumulation* of resources. Rather, they see wealth as the fair *distribution* of resources.

Mahatma Gandhi once articulated this by saying, "Earth provides enough to satisfy every man's needs, but not enough for every man's greed."

Articulate Your Vision

Becoming influential means you have to be able to identify your vision — your compassionate focus. Yet, that focus will stagnate if you cannot articulate it to others in a compelling way. We need the strength of others in order to face the challenges of living out our vision.

This is why building a network around your vision is so important. Influencers grow a group of people who support their vision (and whom they can support). Without the assistance of others, our influence is greatly diminished.

I choose the word "articulate" because sharing your focus means more than just telling it to someone or writing it on a piece of paper. The first three letters of "ARTiculate," capture the essence of how we need to effectively communicate our compassionate focus.

Everyone who has ever influenced others has faced challenges and considered quitting. It was the depth of their purpose that kept them going.

Many advertising consultants would tell you that before developing an advertising strategy you need to remember the 12/7 principle: Your message must have less than 12 words and the customer must see it at least 7 times. But images, music, stories, videos and the arts are far more powerful in conveying a message than the spoken or written word.

This is why, in stating your own compassionate focus you need to use every means of media available. Think of being moved in all of your senses: Sight, sound, taste, touch and smell. Think even more about being moved emotionally.

This is not just important in reaching others — it is just as important in reminding yourself what motivates you. You'll need these images to help sustain you when you face difficult times.

Everyone who has ever influenced others has faced challenges and considered quitting. It was the depth of their purpose that kept them going. Use multiple mediums to deepen your compassionate focus in life.

Everyone who has ever influenced others has faced challenges and considered quitting. It was the depth of their purpose that kept them going.

THE 4EN'S; HABITS OF A COMPELLING LIFE

A compelling life is not incidental — it doesn't happen by accident. Rather, it is very intentional. It is founded upon everyday choices you make to pursue your own compassionate focus. Your are the best person to unfurl the sails and steer the rudder of your future and only you can decide to build the habits of being a compelling person.

The four habits of becoming a compelling person all begin with two letters, "En." In ancient Greek, those two letters describe something going on inside a person. It is very much like our term com-passion — com-pathos, a passion that puts a fire in your belly, unifies your being and unties others around you.

To become a compelling and compassionate person you *must* master these four habits.

1. enCHANT

Enchant comes from the Latin root, en-CANTOS. The term means to sing and specifically to have a song in your heart. Enchanting people put a song in the hearts of the people around them. They have a smile that is infectious and draws people to them. Their joy is obvious, not just on their faces, but in their conversations, e-mails and even their texts.

It is a sincere joy, a habitual joy, a joy that shines beyond sarcasm and merely telling a few jokes. It is seeing the best in others and giving the best of self.

To practice the habit of enCHANTMENT, write down the name of a person you know who might need to be enchanted this week. Include how and when you will contact that individual and what action you will take to enchant him or her.

NAME _____

HOW & WHEN _____

ACTION _____

2. enTHUSE

Enthuse comes from the Greek word for God, "theos." To be enthused is to have the "in-burning fire of God." In ancient Greek, a person who had a compelling spirit possessed an eternal and internal energy, a fire or light that could not be extinguished by any darkness.

I once wrote a song called "Candleflame," the words of the chorus were, "So it (your candle flame) may be weak and feeble, it may small and dim. But the smallest candle still dispels the night. And I will bear it proudly. This tiny, dancing flame. It maybe all I have but it's enough to bring some light. And to a world needing hope it will seem bright."

Your candle doesn't have to be a lighthouse. It just needs to burn consistently — especially where it is darkest.

Another quality that the mot influential people in history have (had) was they always burned their candles where the night was darkest. Rather than fleeing chaos to find peace, they walked into chaos and brought peace.

We bring light to other people's lives through sincerity. Especially when we genuinely listen to others. Listening is a practiced skill. It is not advising, it is not trying to top someone else's story. It is simply drawing out the joy or pain from others by helping them identify what they're feeling.

A substantial amount of research indicates the higher our ability to communicate our emotions, the lower our at-risk behaviors. This applies to adults and to children. I teach this to children as the "Peace Equation."

The higher your wants and the lower your words the more you are likely to hurt (self and others). Here's what the equation looks like:

When WANTS > WORDS the result is hurting behavior.

When WANTS = WORDS the result is healing behavior.

If a child wants a ball but doesn't have the words to express that desire, he or she will just take the ball. If the child has the right words, he or she can ask to share the ball, wait for a turn or request another.

This doesn't just apply to children. If a nation wants a resource (like oil) and doesn't have the ability to reach an agreement diplomatically, they are likely to try and take that resource.

You can raise people's ability to express their emotions by listening sincerely in the following four-step pattern.

a) Identify the FEELING

If you see a person who is frustrated, help them release that frustration by simply identifying the feeling they are exhibiting. The simpler the statement, the better. "You look upset." "You sound excited." "You appear hurt." Then allow him or her time to respond.

b) Encourage the conversation with a simple PHRASE

It need be no more than, "Uh huh." "Please go on." "Do you want to tell me about it?"

Avoid giving advice or asking the person, "Why are you angry / happy / frustrated?" Just encourage them to continue talking.

c) Encourage them with a WISH

Once again the key is simplicity and to stay away from advising. When we advise, we take the power away from the person to create his or her own positive solutions. Initially, their solutions may be steeped in emotion and not at all constructive; "I'm going to kick that person in the derrière." "I'm going to get back at him / her."

People rarely act on those strategies — unless their wants don't match their words. Those phrases are really just a masked attempt to exude emotion. Don't take the bait by trying to argue with that statement; they'll only wind up mad at you for not understanding. If necessary, return to Step 1. "You still sound angry." "You're still feeling hurt, aren't you?"

When you encourage with a wish, you might say something like, "I wish I could have been there at the time." "I wish you had a better experience." "I wish things had worked out differently." "I wish I could have been with you when that happened."

The principal also applies to positive experiences. Many people feel frustrated by joy. That sounds awkward, but expressing our joy is as difficult as expressing our sorrows. Many folks talk incessantly and competitively. We often try to "top" each other's stories. "Well, that's nothing compared to what happened to me."

When you listen, you allow the other person to work through his or her own emotions, come up a personal solution that helps them feel truly acknowledged and affirmed. You help them see their ability to solve issues is already inside of them. We need to avoid the "Savior Complex," when people run to us to solve their problems. It might feed our ego, but it undermines theirs.

d) End with appropriate TOUCH

Unconditional touch is a rare gift these days; almost as rare as a good listener. Touch is so often used to manipulate or control that we can become fearful and resistant to it. To be effective, touch must have no end in mind — no ulterior purpose. Touching simply as a form of affirmation.

To be appropriate, touch must also be in equilibrium with the depth of a relationship. I wouldn't hug a student I'd just met, just as I wouldn't end a deep conversation with my own children with a high-five.

Touch goes from the outside in, as we grow closer to someone. Beginning with the outermost extremity, touch might mean only a handshake. If I know someone a little better, it might involve a pat on the back or shoulder. Rarely is it appropriate to touch someone's face or torso.

Just remember, keep the touch consistent with the relationship. The deeper the relationship, the more you're likely to hug. The newer the relationship, the more your likely to shake a hand or give a high-five. But always use touch to liberate a person, never to manipulate them.

To grow the habit of enCOURAGEMENT, write down the name of a person whom you think needs someone with a gift for listening. Write out how and when you will contact him or her and the action you will take to encourage that individual.

NAME _____

HOW & WHEN _____

ACTION _____

3. enGAGE

Engage comes from a French word meaning, "to make a commitment," to "lead," or to "take a stand."

The primary focus of this book is to help you find the motivating values and inspiring causes to which you will make your own commitment. This will become the a focus that will inspire you to take a stand and become an influential leader — regardless of your position or possessions. However, you don't need to wait until the end of the book to begin taking a stand for others.

With our elementary school program, we tell children, "Don't stand *by*, stand *up!*"

We emphasize that negative behaviors — such a bullying — only exist in a vacuum of pro-social behaviors; behaviors we call "Courageous Choices."

Societally, while we often tell students to stand up for each other, we rarely give them exercises to grow and practice that ability. In our schools we teach a simple three-step process that — when practiced and applied — can be adapted to many areas of anyone's life; including adult bullying behaviors. Here's how it works.

Step 1: Break the cycle

When someone's dignity is being violated, they may not have the capability at the moment to stand up for themselves. You can stand up for them by breaking the cycle of violence that is occurring. Keep in mind that violence is not just physical. Emotional bullying can be as damaging, long lasting and painful as physical bullying.

Whether in a school, at work or on the street, breaking the cycle simply means capturing the attention of the person who is being violated. Sometimes this can be done with a simple touch and by calling the person by name. Help them look in your eyes instead of down at the floor.

You do not have to address the violator at this point. Just break the cycle by getting the victim to look at you instead.

Step 2: Make an Invitation

Invite the victim to do something with you. Go to the library, the lunchroom or out for coffee. The violator will have tried to isolate the victim from protection and his/her bullying behavior is seeking a compliant audience. Move to a different, more positive, public location where the violator will not have the upper hand or an acquiescing audience.

Step 3: Offer a Choice

Before leaving, turn and offer the violator a choice, "Would you like to come with us and do something positive or do you have some place else to go?"

Your choices allow the violator to leave or do something positive. They do not allow the violator to stay and find another victim.

Regardless of the violator's response, walk away with your head held high. You don't have to wait for a response. Whatever choice the violator makes is not your responsibility.

If none of these options work, go find other people to bring into the situation who will not approve of the violator's behavior and not conform to his or her wish for a compliant audience. Again, the violator is looking for control and an audience. Bringing together other people who disapprove of his/her behavior immediately changes the equation. To grow the habit of enGAGEMENT, list two people you could teach these three steps and practice the behaviors with them. Have one person play the role of the violator, the second the victim and you be the enGAGER. Then create another scenario and trade roles. Do this until everyone has had a chance to practice these behaviors. Ask your friends to go teach two others — pay it forward.

Person 1: _____

Person 2: _____

Scenario 1: _____

_____

Scenario 2: _____

_____

Scenario 3: _____

_____

4. enCOURAGE

Encourage comes from the French word "couer," meaning heart. An encouraging person puts strength in someone else's heart. The best way to be enCOURaging is through simple acts of intentional COURtesy. Nothing gives more courage to others then when you go out of your way to be kind — especially to someone who is the least accepted or most rejected. With our little ones, we call this the pyramid of Intentional Courtesy:

1. Go out of your way

2. To be kind

3. To the lonely, sad and even the mad.

The level of a relationship can be measured by the courtesy in that relationship. Relationships thrive when courtesy thrives and they just as quickly die when courtesy dies. The same applies to communities. Communities thrive when courtesy is an intentional focus and die when courtesy is absent.

I've visited thousands of businesses and schools in my years. In all that time, I've learned to spot the level of trust in these places within a matter of minutes. Simply by watching the level of courtesy between administration and staff, staff and staff, staff and customer (students/parents).

To grow your ability to enCOURage others, practice the habit of specifically complimenting someone who is often rejected or not accepted by others. I use the word "specific" because a general compliment can often undermine someone's trust in you. If used too often or if untied to specific behavior, the recipient can grow to distrust your sincerity.

Making a specific compliment means finding out enough about a person to see what matters to him or her and to identify how they are growing in that area. However, nothing is more powerful and motivating to a person than a specific compliment.

Name:_____

_____

Specific Compliment:_____

_____

_____

You can also grow your ability to enCOURage by expressing your gratitude to others. Again, the more specific the compliment, the more powerful the result. Identify a person who has been encouraging in your life. Purchase or create a card and write — in your personal handwriting — why you are grateful to that person.

Instead of sending the card, ask to see the person. Read the card out loud to them and then give it to him or her. The result will deeply impact both of you.

Name:_____

Why you are grateful: _____

_____

_____

When will you meet?

  Date and Time:_____

  Location: _____

THE ANTI-EN THAT WILL STEAL YOUR ENERGY

The one "En" word you do not see on this list is "enTERTAIN." As in, "Entertain me."

The root of this word is to divert or amuse. To say, "Entertain me," is to expect others to divert or amuse you. Though there are definitely times we need to divert and amuse ourselves, it becomes a problem when we don't keep these diversions or amusements in moderation. Being entertained reduces our capacity to be compelling or compassionate when:

1. We seek diversion or amusement over a meaningful focus in our lives.

2. We expect others to be responsible for our entertainment.

In my own life I've always addressed this as the difference between *"being bored,"* and *"being boring."*

Life is so full of opportunities, if I say, "I'm bored," it is an indication of my inability to be creative and engaged. It is not the responsibility of others to entertain me. It is my responsibility to engage life. The sooner I absorb that lesson, the more my life will have meaning.

Being bored — being entertained — becomes a very negative habit and compulsion in our lives. We need to root it out and replace it with the compelling habits of enCHANT, enTHUSE, enCOURAGE and enGAGE.

90 DAYS TO A NEW LIFE

Habits are difficult to build — but only for the first 90 days. After 90 days, your body actually begins to long for the behavior. This applies to habits — which are positive — or compulsions — which are negative.

It applies whether I am building new eating habits, study habits or workout habits. Many people quit new endeavors within a few days or weeks, but if you hang in there for just three months — you will have grown a deep, new, positive way of living. 90 days is a very short commitment when it can bring you a lifetime of joy.

As you read through rest of this book, you will learn to identify the habits, values and focus you want to grow in your life.

Activity 1.1 Unifying Purpose

Before you read on, talk, e-mail or text three people whom you think have a unifying purpose. Ask each person what his or her purpose might be and how it has affected their lives. Write down the name of the person, the high points of the conversations and their unifying (compassionate) purpose.

The information on these forms will be used later in Chapter 3 when you begin developing your own compassionate focus.

Example:

Inspiring People I Know: My Father

What Inspired Them?: Serving his country, his mother who although a single mom was committed to his education, his decision to go to Harvard, become a professor and share his knowledge with others around the world.

Name:

What Inspired Them? _____

_____

_____

Name:_____

What Inspired Them? _____

_____

_____

Name:_____

What Inspired Them? _____

_____

_____

Activity 1.2 Influential People

Influence is not tied to a position (having authority, political or corporate office) or possessions (money, the things you own). Indeed, some of the most influential people in history shunned both. Let's take a moment to consider some of history's influential people who shunned position and possessions.

1. Make a note of some of the most influential people in the world who shunned position and possessions.

2. Identify location, primary cause or focus and at least one famous quote.

Example:

Name of Influential Person: Chief Joseph

Location, Primary Cause or Focus, Quote: Northwest US and Canada. Sought to prevent war and keep his people from being forced to live on a reserve.

Name:_____

Location, Primary Cause or Focus, Quote:

Name:_____

Location, Primary Cause or Focus, Quote:

Name:_____

Location, Primary Cause or Focus, Quote:

Activity 1.3 The Gratitude List

A great way to start focusing on what you can do and what you do have is to build a gratitude list. This is a simple list with great power. Make a note of specifics acts or people for whom you are grateful. We will call this the "I am blessed," list. Then make another note writing down the things you have done to help others. Let's call this the "I have blessed," list. Don't just use this list once, keep it near you and continually grow it.

In ancient Greek there were two words for blessing. One was "blessed," *Makarios*. Which meant, "You are so fortunate," or, "The gods must favor you."

The other word was "blessing," *Eulogio*. Which meant, "What did you do with your life (or good fortune)?"

We received the word, eulogy, from eulogio. A eulogy is no more than a five to ten minute summary of a person's entire life. "What you did with what you had..."

How can you turn your makarios (luck), into a eulogy (a great summary of your life)? Create a cycle of blessed and blessing in your life; a cycle of how can you be blessed and become a blessing. When I teach children we often say, "We are blessed to bless others," or, "We are loved to love others."

Continually add to this list and during those times, when you feel frustrated or fragile, review this list and it will give you incredible power to pursue your focus.

Gratitude List

_____   _____

_____   _____

_____   _____

_____   _____

_____   _____

_____   _____

_____   _____

_____   _____

_____   _____

_____   _____

_____   _____

_____   _____

_____   _____

Activity 1.4 Question-Ectomies

Come up with three different scenarios that have happened to you; times when you wished you had responded differently to a challenge you faced. Change the question from a negative to a positive one.

Question-Ectomies

Cut out the negative question   Replace it with a positive action.

Scenario	Negative Question	Positive Action
I lost my cool with an associate today	*Why can't I control my temper?*	*I am going to take some quiet time each morning before I go to work and I'm going to ask my associate to forgive me and ask him out to lunch.*

Activity 1.5 Inspiring Media

I am loved	To love others
What others have done for me	*What I have done for others*

Example

My son sent me a kind text saying, "I miss you dad."	I filled out a compliment card for a waitperson who provided exceptional service.

As you develop your own Compassionate Focus and Values Statement in the following chapter, begin a collection of video clips, movies, songs and images that inspire you.

Take a moment now to find at least three pieces of media that inspire you.

PERSON _____

MEDIA(Quote, Picture, Painting, Video Clip, Music)

_____

_____

_____

_____

CAUSE_____

MEDIA (Quote, Picture, Painting, Video Clip, Music)

_____

_____

_____

_____

II
Values

Values: Your Guiding Star
Behavioral Triangulation

For hundreds of years, explorers used the stars to guide them on voyages. Now, we use GPS (Global Positioning Systems) to show us our location anytime we can access satellite communication. A GPS triangulates your position by locating it in relationship to three points, including the satellite. Our values are similar. They help us identify our "behavioral location" by triangulating our actions according to three points 1) How we expect to be treated, 2) how we will treat others and 3) those behaviors and expectations we will display regardless of our circumstances.

> **Values define: 1) How we expect to be treated, 2) how we will treat others and 3) those behaviors and expectations we will display regardless of our circumstances.**

The opposite of values are situational ethics, we might even call them conveniences; changing our behavior based on what is momentarily expedient. This includes "situational conveniences" — changing my behavior based upon the situation — and "interpersonal conveniences" — changing my behavior based upon the people around me.

An example of a situational convenience would be some-one who acts one way when surrounded by people he or she knows, but changes that behavior when feeling anonymous. Let's say a person is polite to others when he is at church, a professional meeting, or school, then climbs into his car and starts cutting people off in traffic while screaming obscenities at those around him.

An example of an interpersonal convenience is when an individual changes her or his behavior to impress others. For example, acting respectfully in front of an authority figure, then later speaking poorly behind that person's back so as to im-press one's peers.

When you think of *values*, think of *maturity*. The two are in-separable. People acting like adolescents make decisions based upon the circumstances or people around them. Mature people articulate their values and then make important decisions — including relational choices — based upon those values.

By this definition, we see maturity is not *chronological*; it is *be-havioral*. A 16-year-old who decides not to go to a party, because she knows there will be alcohol present, is much more mature than a 50-year-old who goes into debt buying a car or truck only because it will, "impress the neighbors."

Using this definition, we can't mature without first articulat-ing our values (so we can make decisions based upon them). The primary focus of this chapter is to help you further ar-ticulate your values into a personal values statement that will guide you in good times and bad.

The "No Matter What" Factor

The main catchphrase of a value is this: It is how you will be-have "no matter what..."

No matter what others are doing... No matter what you *could* get away with... No matter whether others are watching... No matter what...

See Activity 2.1

What is the importance of a value?

Values offer two major functions in your life:

1. Values guide your behavior and decisions in all areas of your life: Educational, financial, physical, professional, recreational, relational and spiritual.

2. Values strengthen your resolve when you are under negative pressure from peers, emotional distress, or even cultural messages that may be contrary to what you believe.

A great role model of the sustaining power of a value was the Farm Worker turned Civil Rights leader, César Chavéz. He was a Mexican-American farm worker raised in poverty. His parents owned a store and land but lost it during the Great Depression. In exchange for the deed on a new farm, César's father cleared eighty acres of land by hand. Sadly, after he cleared it the agreement was broken and the land was taken from him. The original owner then purchased the acreage back for an obscenely low amount.

Eventually, the family moved to California where the parents and children worked as farm laborers just to meet their basic needs. César himself had to leave school at eleven to work in the fields and only received a third grade education.

Instead of choosing anger or hopelessness, César's commitment to the rights of those around him led him to become a non-violent leader of farm workers around the world. His deep commitments not only to faith, nonviolence, but also to the rights of the working poor, led Presidential Medal of Honor winner, Robert Kennedy, to visit César on one of his hunger fasts for human rights. Kennedy said this about Mr. Chavéz; "I am here out of respect for one of the heroic figures of our time – César Chavéz. I congratulate all of you who are locked with César in the struggle for justice for the farm worker and in the struggle for justice for Spanish-speaking Americans."

Chavéz's favorite statement was, "Sí, se puede," which loosely translates into, "Yes, it can be done."

He focused on what *could* be done — not what *couldn't*. He chose to grow the resources he *did* have to work with — not what he *didn't*. He stood by his values of compassion and human dignity all of his life and in the process left an indelible mark on the world. Those core values gave Chavéz the strength to sustain his vision despite great opposition and the ability to not react negatively to the fierce hostility he often faced. His values guided his behavior and strengthened his resolve.

Identifying my values

We don't necessarily learn our core values from classes on ethics, morals or religion. We learn *what* we value by *who* values us. César Chavez no doubt learned his values of hard work and persistence watching his father and mother make ends meet no matter how dire their situation. Critical to learning our values, we also have to learn the difference between someone who *values* us and someone who is *using* us — manipulating us.

When people manipulate you, they see you merely as a *means* to their *ends*. You're merely an actor on their stage. They will use whatever behaviors are necessary to coerce you to do what they want, regardless of whether it would be best for you in the long run.

When people manipulate you, they see you merely as a *means* to their *ends*.

Another sure sign of manipulation is that someone who is manipulating you will try to isolate you from the ones who truly value you. They don't want people who care about you to question the way they are treating you or what they are trying to get you to do.

For thirty years, I've worked with young people involved in gangs. Often, they tell me they find acceptance, belonging and purpose in the gang. But the price is high. They have to do whatever the gang leaders say; carry drugs for them, have sex with the leaders, fight for the leaders turf, even go to prison for them.

If you cross these leaders, they may kill you and they'll rarely let you walk away without paying a heavy price. Beatings are common and many people do not survive.

They'll give initiates new names, Coyote, Lion or Spider, not because they want to grow your character — but because they want to grow your dependence. They don't want you to remember your old self. People who manipulate you don't want to see you more independent, but constantly more dependent upon them.

The opposite is true when someone values you. They always want the best for you. They don't try to isolate you from people who have your best interest at heart. In fact, they'll try to help you grow positive relationships. They want your independence; they want you to be able to meet your own needs and form your own healthy friendships.

Manipulation can be described as "performance-based approval."

"I will give you my approval if you do what I want."

Gang leaders would be extreme examples of people offering performance-based approval. However most examples of manipulation are far more subtle and difficult to recognize. For example, the parent who withdraws their love when you don't live up to their expectation.

Sadly, many people don't recognize this as manipulation and either use this type of behavior or have been a victim of it much of their life. Sadly, we seek the approval of the parent least likely to give it, something which can haunt people all their lives.

The opposite of manipulation — when someone truly values you — is unconditional dignity. These are people in your life who always seek your dignity — even when you don't. They want the best for you... "No matter what..."

When someone values you they treat you with unconditional dignity.

Neurosurgeon, Dr. Ben Carson, is the Director of Pediatric Neurosurgery at Johns Hopkins Hospital. He was also awarded the Presidential Medal of Honor, the highest civilian award in the United States.

Dr. Carson was the first surgeon to successfully separate two Siamese twins conjoined at the back of the head (working with a 70-member surgical team for 22 hours).

Dr. Carson's life wasn't always so stellar. Raised in Detroit, Michigan, he struggled with poor grades and anger management throughout elementary school. During a school fight, Dr. Carson punched another student in the face with a padlock (from a school locker). The resulting wound required stitches and Ben was nearly expelled.

It was Ben's mom, Sonya — a single-mother working tirelessly to provide for her two boys — that believed in Ben, even when Ben gave up on himself.

Despite the fact his mother was unable to read, she limited the children's television watching to thirty minutes a week and made them read at least two books weekly, reporting the content back to her.

Dr. Carson's mom loved him unconditionally. The result was a man who has changed pediatric neurosurgery and influenced the lives of many.

Ben Carson learned his values from someone who unconditionally valued him — his mother. It doesn't mean she was always nice either. Those who value us will also challenge us to pursue rigorous standards for our own life. It's not that they expect us to be the best, but they do expect us to do our best.

Growing my values

We *grow* our values by *valuing* others.

There is only one way to grow a value — practice it habitually until it becomes part of your core being.

Begin practicing your values in a safe place around those you trust. Then, to grow them exponentially, apply your values by standing up for what you believe in challenging and difficult situations.

> There is only one way to grow a value — practice it habitually until it becomes part of your core being.

According to the theory of Cognitive Dissonance, we *become* how we *behave*. If what we believe conflicts with how we behave, guess which will change? Our beliefs or our behaviors?

If you deduced, "beliefs," you were right. If there is a dissonance between how we believe and how we behave, we'll change our beliefs. That is why some children can be brought up in wonderful environments but then begin changing their character during their adolescent years.

A good definition of adolescence would be to compare it to a child with a suitcase full of masks. The child tries on multiple masks until they find the one that gets the most attention. Then they keep using that mask until it hardens. It is not about approval, it is about attention. We become what receives attention.

To a person stuck in adolescence, primary attention begins to come from peers rather than adults. Even more so in a culture where children spend a significant portion of their day in large groups overseen by only one adult. In those situations, the adults are not largely building relationships with the children as much as they are imparting information. Values, which are caught not taught, are not the priority. Nor is a lot of the attention received from adults positive. But positive or negative, attention is attention and we long for it.

This can work *for* us or *against* us.

We can decide who will mentor us. Who will attend to us and for what we will receive attention. If I have high ideals but am constantly compromising my values to succumb to the whims of those around mw; my ideals will be undermined.

Alternatively, if I set high standards and place myself in positions where I am consistently practicing those values — my beliefs will change to affirm my actions.

Whatever values I seek to deepen, it is important to remember the 90-day rule mentioned in Chapter 1. It takes at least 90 days for any behavior or value to become a habit or belief.

Identifying my values?

You've already taken a huge step in articulating your core values in Activity 2.1. Remember the two statements we made earlier in this chapter?

- We learn *what* we value by *who* values us, and
- We *grow* our values by *valuing* others.

Now we're going to work at articulating the most important values in your life. Beliefs that will sustain you and actions that will empower you *no matter what*... No matter what circumstance you're in. No matter what the people around you are doing.

See Activity 2.2 and then move on to Activity 2.3

Activity 2.1 No Matter What

Take a moment and journal about the following two topics.
On one side of the paper, write how you want others to treat
you — "no matter what." On the other side make a correlating
statement about how you will treat others "no matter what."

Values: The "No-Matter-What" Factor

How do I expect to be treated, "No matter what..."	How I will treat others, "No Matter What..."
I want people to look for my dignity, even when I make mistakes. I want them to see I am doing my best.	*I will look for the best in others, complimenting them when they are doing well and encouraging them when they make mistakes. Mistakes are a sign we're still trying...*

Activity 2.2 Identify Your Values

Fill out the following chart entitled, "Identify Your Values."

Take time to talk to the people you identified in questions 1 and 2. If that is not possible, talk to someone who supports you about the people you have named. Walking through this section with a mentor will deepen the impact of the values you are listing.

The key questions are:

1. On the following sheet, name three people older than you that have valued you. Write or tell a story about how each person helped you feel valued.

2. Name three people who are younger than you whom you have valued. Write or tell a story about how you helped each person feel valued.

3. Identify common themes between what those who value you want for your life and what you want for those whom you value. Avoid general words such as happiness or success. Instead, identify the components of happiness or success to the people you've named. Examples might include wisdom, compassion, health, financial independence and/or caring relationships.

4. Circle three words that are key values to you.

Identify Your Values

Do this exercise with someone who values you. Share stories together about the people who have valued you both during your lives.

PART 1

Name someone older than you who valued you (sought your dignity, "no matter what." Tell a story about when you felt valued by that person.	Name someone around your age or younger that you value. Tell a story about when you helped that person feel valued.
My Swim Coach, pushed me to be MY best, wasn't worried if I wasn't THE best	*My children, it doesn't matter to me what they DO in life, what matters to me is that they find meaning.*

PART 2

1. Identify common themes between the way you want to be treated unconditionally and the way you will treat others. Avoid such general words as happiness or success. For example a medical professional might want to be treated as professional, competent and collaborative. Choosing the right words for you matters deeply as these words will be your GPS, guiding your behavior at all times. Other examples might be wisdom, compassion or engaging. Write down at least nine words below.

_____   _____   _____

_____   _____   _____

_____   _____   _____

2. Now, circle three of the words above that are THE most important to you.

PART 3

ARTiculating my values

We stated previously that a written or verbal values statement is not nearly as impacting as stating something artistically.

One of the best ways to share your values is through an artistic values statement placed upon a laminated business card.

Let's look at some values statements of people who were very influential throughout history.

- "When you were born, you cried and the world rejoiced. Live your life so that when you die, the world cries and you rejoice." — White Elk, 1181/1182 to 1226
- "As we let our own light shine, we unconsciously give other people permission to do the same." — Nelson Mandela, Born, 1918
- "You must be the change you wish to see in the world." — Mohandes Gandhi, 1869-1948
- "I have a dream that my four little children will one day live in a nation where they will not be judged by the color of their skin but by the content of their character." — Rev. Dr. Martin Luther King, Jr., August 28, 1963
- "Spread love everywhere you go. Let no one ever come to you without leaving happier." — Mother Teresa, 1910 to 1997

Activity 2.3
Articulate Your Own Values Statement

Before we create our own values statement, we must follow a few parameters for maximum effectiveness.

1. In order to commit a statement to working memory, it is ideal to write a comprehensible sentence of less than 12 words.

2. Take your top 3 values from the list you made in Activity 2.2.

3. Make a motivational sentence (a sentence that moves you to action), incorporating those 3 top values. Use post-it notes to rearrange the words until you find a combination that is meaningful to you.

4. Download a business card template and insert your values statement on that card along with a place for your signature and date.

5. Download a graphic that is symbolic or important to you and insert it in the background on the template.

6. Print 12 cards or more, sign and date them then have them laminated.

7. Keep one card in a wallet or purse (with you at all times). Put one on your bed stand at home. Read it before you sleep and after you wake. Tape one to your mirror. If you have a book or journal, keep one card inside it. Give extra cards to friends who value you and whom you know will support you in living by your values statement.

Let's use an example of a young man who created the following values statement (I'll change his name to I.B. Amazing).

His three primary values were:

1. Laughter
2. Compassion
3. Hope.

The sentence he crafted was,

"Through laughter, I act with compassion bringing hope to all I meet."

He then took a picture of himself jumping joyfully in the air and downloaded the jpeg file to his business card template (the picture is changed as well — but you'll get the idea).

To the left is what his final business card / values statement looked like.

Do you remember what we discussed earlier about adolescence and maturity?

- Adolescence lasts as long as your peers define your self-esteem.
- Maturity begins when you have the ability to articulate your values and make life choices by them — including those with whom you will build relationships.

This is an opportunity to articulate your values clearly and succinctly. Put the effort into it so your values statement can become the GPS that will help steer your life at all times — both consciously and subconsciously.

Give your Values Card to people who unconditionally value you. Ask them to check in with you on a regular basis to see how you are growing your values or even to share stories about when you found those values deepening in your life.

Their support will be one of the behaviors that deepen your beliefs.

III
Compassionate Focus

Your Compassionate Focus

Com-Passion "a Unifying (com) Drive (Pathos)"

Imagine greeting each morning with enthusiasm, eager to jump into each day, excited about who you will see and what you will be doing. No, it is not because of a new pill or stimulant on the market. Nor, is it because you feel the first faint hints of spring love. It is because you have a Compassionate Focus; a unifying drive to make a difference in the world.

Founding director of RandomKid.org, Talia Leman feels this kind of zest for life. It didn't begin with passion as much as compassion. She was watching the events of Hurricane Katrina unfold before her and the countless numbers of people left homeless while the government seemed unable to respond left her stunned.

Stunned, but not speechless.

Immediately, Talia went to work, encouraging her friends to collect funds for Katrina's victims instead of candy for themselves on that fateful Halloween of 2005. When her plea went viral on social media, the money began rolling in — $10.5 million US altogether. A little over a million dollars for every year, Talia had lived. She was just over ten years old when she began her effort.

Spurred by the response, Talia started RandomKid.org and turned her focus to a new cause, that of educating young females in developing countries.

She focused on areas where the girls could not attend school because they spent the majority of their days carrying water for miles from unsanitary sources. This also exposed them to diseases flourishing both in the water and the insects around it.

To date, Talia's efforts have resulted in over 350 schools, all with wells attached. Each well driven — not by a gas or electric pump — but by a merry-go-round. When the children play at recess, they are also pumping clean, free water.

Compassion prompted Talia to begin her work, a quality that is the opposite of pity. Pity begins by seeing a problem in the world and ends by feeling sorry for those involved. Compassion sees a challenge in the world and looks at effective ways to respond. It is compassion that's kept Talia focused all these years.

Here is an example of the difference between pity and compassion. Many years ago, I volunteered at an orphanage in Mexican Baja region. I can remember being in the yard and working on basic math with a small group of children. It was too hot inside and we were working in the yard using the dirt as a chalkboard.

As we were working a Recreational Vehicle the size of a trailer house pulled up to the gate of the yard. A man came around to the mid-cabin door with a camera. He popped the door open and a woman began emptying bags of candy into the dirt by the RV.

Immediately the children jumped up from the learning circle and dove into the dirt for candy. All the while, the man was snapping pictures of the cacophony.

I've no doubt the man and woman thought they were being compassionate, but their work was based in pity. Instead of raising the dignity of the children they turned them into beggars.

Compassion begins with a feeling, but it turns into inquiry and then into effective action, action that builds dignity instead of taking it away

Compassion begins with a feeling, but it turns into inquiry and then into effective action, action that builds dignity instead of taking it away. Actions without inquiry often disable people instead of empowering them. To try to change someone without knowing them — or a system without knowing the people it affects — is violent.

Talia's actions grew from analysis of the situation and then a childlike response that lacked any fear of failure. Her original goal was $100 dollars for Katrina Relief. Her result was $10.5 million dollars.

A compassionate focus sustains our efforts, transcends our fears and engages our being. The deeper my compassionate focus, the more I am engaged. For the ultimate energized life, grow your compassionate focus.

THE INTERSECTION OF FOUR POWERFUL FORCES

Some people might call Talia's success *lucky*. They would be wrong. Talia's success is part of the energy that still drives her. Her bright outlook on life is contagious; she is enchanting, engaging, encouraging and, of course, enthusiastic.

Talia is *lucky* only in the sense that she created the conditions for her own success. She had a compassionate focus, she articulated it and built a network of caring people around that focus. This is a formula for "luck" that has been used by every person of influence in history and is still used by influential people.

That formula includes four ingredients:

1. Influential people can articulate *what* moves them and *who* inspires them.

2. They know what personality traits (*strengths*) make them unique.

3. They employ the *talents* or *skills* that make them great.

4. They seek out people who will *support* them in pursuing their focus.

Together, the four ingredients combine into a singular Compassionate Focus; a driving force that becomes increasingly powerful the more you pursue it.

If you want to wake up each morning enthusiastic about what lies ahead, whom you will see and what you are doing, then defining your own Compassionate Focus will be the "lucky ticket" for your personal well of inspiration.

COMPASSIONATE FOCUS AND VALUES STATEMENT

You might wonder how your Compassionate Focus will differ from your Values Statement. In this comprehensive approach, we'll actually see how they blend together. If you think of yourself as the Captain of your own boat on a long voyage across the ocean, your Values Statement would be your sextant (we've used the contemporary term, a GPS), telling you where you are at all times on your journey.

By comparison, your Compassionate Focus tells you your direction; the course you want to set in your life. Your Values Statement tells you your *position*, your Compassionate Focus tells you your *direction*.

Your Values Statement tells you your position, your Compassionate Focus tells you your direction.

I'm very careful here not to say that it is your plan or destination. There are notable differences between a direction, a plan and a destination.

Often people become stuck planning their destinations and miss all the beauty along the way. They work up detailed 1, 2, or 5-year strategies around these plans. It is like going on a vacation and having every moment planned to the minutest detail. Then, they return exhausted from trying to keep themselves or others in control and on track.

It is easy to forget life has it's own ebbs and tides, wind shifts and weather changes. Creating detailed yearlong strategies may help us feel in control, but it pours our energy into the wrong cup; *managing* our plans instead of *directing* our lives.

Joy comes from choosing a direction and then having the flexibility to respond to the changes around us. When the wind changes or a challenge comes our way, a person with a compulsive plan will ask; "Why does this always happen to me?" Feeling like life has thrown a curve at them.

In reality, life is ever changing and the rate of change in our world is growing exponentially. The true condition of life is not homeostasis but constant transformation. We spend inordinate amounts of energy trying to keep things stable. What we don't realize is that, in so doing, we're fighting a universe, not just an issue.

Trying to constantly live in a state of equilibrium is like trying to swim upstream to reach the ocean. Instead, identify your direction and let the river carry you down.

A high need for control (of others or self) correlates with a fear of change. Learning to live by your values and creating a direction from your Compassionate Focus will not only decrease the *fear* in your life, but also increase the *joy*.

Follow the steps and don't rush through this part of the guide. Think of this chapter (not so much as a task you must check off) but an opportunity to continually renew your direction in life. This guide is a process — not a destination.

Like life, your Compassionate Focus will be a dynamic endeavor. It will grow with you. The more you "play with it," the more it will "work for you."

> **Like life, your Compassionate Focus will be a dynamic endeavor. It will grow with you. The more you "play with it," the more it will "work for you."**

The worst thing you could do is treat your compassionate focus like some people treat a degree. Once they've earned it, they pretend to be the expert with nothing left to learn. The greatest minds don't strive to be experts in their field; they don't pretend to know all there is to know in their field, they seek to be in *awe* of what they still have to *learn*.

Seek to increase your *expertise* without becoming an *expert*. People who are life-long learners, like Albert Einstein, see the goal of knowledge is mystery, not answers. They are less concerned about the right answers than the right questions. Remember what we said when studying Question-Ectomies; "If you ask the wrong question, you'll always get the wrong response. Once you think you have all the answers, your own mindset will keep you from being open to new discoveries and creativity.

Einstein was thought of as "dull" in school, he had a series of jobs, none of which suited him. His father, Hermann, passed away when Albert was in his early twenties and died thinking his son would amount to nothing.

Eventually, Albert found a job as a clerk working in a patent office. It was from there — as a total outsider to the physics community — that Albert wrote his two most well-known formulas on matter and time.

One of Einstein's most well known quotes was, "Creativity is more important than knowledge."

He saw science as a playground and physics as an open opportunity to wonder.

Look at your Compassionate Focus in the same light. It will become a springboard to a lifetime of learning that will help you expand your mind, body and spirit for the rest of your joyful life.

There will be five sections to your compassionate focus.

1. Your Values Statement
2. What causes move you and what people inspire you?
3. What are your unique personality strengths?
4. What gifts and talents would you like to master?
5. Who will support you in growing your values and compassionate focus?

After examining each area find articles, quotes, video clips, or artistic examples (stories, plays, books, paintings, sculptures, songs or photographs),that relate to those sections.

We're going to be spending more time talking to these supportive people as we develop your Compassionate Focus. This is the start of building a network around your vision. It will be the foundation for building a community of support that will sustain you — especially in the preliminary stage of pursuing your Compassionate Focus.

I heard an engineer say that a Space Shuttle would burn up 80% of its fuel in the first 10 miles of the mission. It takes that much energy just to get out of the earth's atmosphere and gravitational pull.

Similarly, most of your energy will be in the initial steps of re-orienting your life towards your new vision. There will be old habits to break and maybe even relationships from which you need to distance yourself (because they're either demeaning or manipulative).

The best way to break the bonds of a negative habit is *Replacement Theory*. Instead of focusing on the old, negative habit (or relationship); focus on replacing it with something positive. That is exactly what you'll be doing as you build strong relationships around vibrant habits.

Start building your network now.

Q1: WHAT causes move you and WHO inspires you

When we begin filling out the four quadrants of your compassionate focus we will first examine what you are passionate about — the *causes that move* you and the *people who inspire* you. Take quality time to complete this section and — once you complete it — don't worry if you need to change it over time.

1. Causes

Many of us have seen events or circumstances in the world that moved us on an emotional level. Sometimes, because the issues are so large, we turn away or hope "someone will do something."

Let those causes free in this exercise.

Causes might include Water Poverty or poverty in general, they might be related to people or the earth; environmental deterioration, resource depletion or socioeconomic injustice, prejudice or violence.

They might be local issues such as homelessness or recycling or international issues like malaria and AIDS.

Ask people who've known you over time if they've noticed you moved by certain issues or causes.

Capture the essence of the cause and why it moves you. Write that out in words so you can see it concretely.

2. Inspirers

Think of people who have inspired you throughout your life. These people might be historic such as Sitting Bull or Nelson Mandela or they might be personal to you, a parent, teacher or coach.

List these people and why they've moved you. What it is they offered to your life and what qualities do they have that inspired you.

Start a file on your computer where you can capture images, video clips, quotes or other inspiring media dealing with the causes that move you and the people who inspire you. This will be important for two reasons.

- You will be able to turn to this information at times you lose your focus and feel discouraged or overburdened.
- This information will become part of your Positive Social Profile leading like-minded people to network with you and deepen your influence in the world.

The keys to being an influential person are 1) Managing your own Mentors and 2) planning your week by *who* you need to see more than *what* you need to do.

The more influential you are, the more you will spend your week building your network rather than thinking of your tasks. If your *task list* is larger than your *network list* your influence doesn't extend beyond your reach. You will be too busy managing daily tasks to increase your influence.

As you expand your network, you will have other people who will be motivated to help with your tasks. Now, your influence will be measured by the number of other influential people you know and the power of their networks.

Managing your Mentors builds from this principle. We can choose the people who will influence our lives, support our values and deepen our compassionate focus. Indeed, this is the greatest tool you can use to leverage your future.

This is a key element to raising an entrepreneurial generation or becoming entrepreneurial ourselves. It's not the information retained — information is easy to access — that will build our future. It is the ability to articulate a purpose and build a network around it.

This needs to become a core aspect of our school's curriculum if this generation is going to be able to compete in an innovative world (beyond an industrial or information society). Who you know will be more important than what you know, but forming a sustainable community-of-purpose will be the primary task of this generation.

This should not be something we hope children learn. It is something they must learn. It will take a substantial effort to reconfigure education to initiate this change. Largely because most educators have been in the field the vast majority of their lives. Their advancement was related to how much information they could retain and then impart. This new agenda will call them to think beyond disseminating information and into the creative application of information.

Q2: What Personality Strengths Make You Unique?

Quadrant 2 focuses on what personality traits (strengths) make you unique — Who are you great at *being* (as opposed to what are you great at *doing*)?

Many of us flinch when someone tells us we are "unique." That's because the term is frequently used in a negative context as if it is wrong to be nonconformist or eccentric in any circumstance.

From early ages, we are pushed to *conform* to peer pressure or *comply* with adult pressure and the people who are most manipulative or demand the greatest compliance are those who have the greatest fear of losing control. That fear overwhelms their whole outlook on life and relationships with other people.

In reality, nothing makes us more human than the infinite possibilities we have to be distinctly and individually remarkable.

At least three aspects go into distinguishing us as individuals. Our IQ, EQ, and Personalities.

1. IQ: Intelligence Quotient

The impact of IQ on your life is quite debatable. Standard IQ tests have been widely used to measure intelligence since the First World War. Increasingly, research indicates these tests measure how one will do in *education* more than how one will do in their *personal* or *professional* life. Such tests may only measure a specific type of intelligence and might also be culturally biased.

Current education practice tends to reward those who learn by listening and reading. A growing body of research tells us the group of people who retain knowledge solely in this manner is quite small, smaller still when retention of knowledge is attached to frequent testing. Why? Because, in such environments, the brain only stores information in short-term memory and erases it upon completion of the test. Memorization without application is not learning.

People have multiple styles of learning — touch, sight, hearing, movement, discussion and every combination thereof — the list is as varied as our personalities and senses.

Adele Diamond, a professor at the University of British Columbia and one of the foremost neuroscientists who study the science of how the brain actually learns, says that no matter how we receive knowledge, we don't learn it unless we play with it. She states this is true for all mammals, including the human variety.

No matter how we receive knowledge, we don't *learn* it unless we *play* with it

We play with knowledge when we do something *creative* with the information we receive.

While your IQ may be locked at a certain level, your ability to learn information by playing with it is nearly infinite. This becomes even more important as we age. Once past 40, the myelin sheath that surrounds the neurons in the brain begins to deteriorate. These sheaths are like an Internet cable losing its insulation. As that occurs, the information traveling through the cable diffuses and the reception weakens.

Similarly, as our myelin sheath weakens so does the information we retain. To supplement that biological occurrence, neuroscientists suggest we strengthen our capacity to create and play. What we earlier referred to as "Transient Hypofrontality" — interrupting the automatic cycle of "thought / behavior," and letting the brain wander.

Sadly, a high outcomes focus in education misses the value of play focusing instead of memorization and recitation of information. We do away with recess, the arts, music and physical exercise — all areas where the brain can be most creative. The focus shifts to short-term test scores instead of long-term application in an entrepreneurial economy.

That, however, should not limit *your* ability to learn by playing with new information. When you learn something new, you can commit it to long-term memory by playing with it. Playing can be as varied as having a conversation about the new knowledge, make a skit out of it, turn it into a poem, or put it into some other form of art. Find a way to practice and apply it during your day and look at it from multiple angles. *Play with it.*

Even what (how) we need to learn in order to excel in this global economy is surrounded by controversy today. With an increasing amount of information at our fingertips, it becomes less important *what* we learn and ever-more-important to "learn *how* to learn."

In his book, "A Whole New Mind," author and lecturer, Daniel Pink, says the five most important *intelligences* we must develop today are design, story, symphony, empathy, play and meaning (Penguin Books, 2005).

Howard Gardner, Dean of Harvard Business School, highlights a very similar list; discipline, synthesis, creative, respectful, and ethical (Harvard Business School Press, 2006).

Combining the lists we find multiple similarities. Almost all the advances in the fields of medicine, technology, engineering and other areas occur at the crossroads between disciplines, the *synthesis* and *application* of information. For example the fMRI (functional Magnetic Resonating Imaging), which combine technology and neuroscience to see not just how the brain looks but essentially how the brain works.

Almost all the advances in the fields of medicine, technology, engineering and other areas occur at the crossroads between disciplines, the *synthesis* and *application* of information.

These advances only occur when entrepreneurial minds see how both ideas and people can be connected into an applicable whole. This is important, the very definition neuroscientists (who focus in this area) use for creativity is the Three U's; results must be Unique, Unexpected and Utilitarian.

If the information created is inapplicable, then it doesn't fit the creative category. Application of ideas is critical to creativity.

Once again, we return to a statement we made at the very beginning of this guide. Your influence is directly attached to your ability to articulate a compassionate focus and to build a community around it. Your IQ Score is far less important than your ability to apply and play with new knowledge, then motivate a group of people to act on it.

2. EQ: Emotional Quotient

A few years ago, I was asked to eulogize my mother at her funeral. In the short window available to summarize my mother's life to her gathered family and friends, I chose to say my mother saw people *telescopically*, not *microscopically*.

She saw the potential in people, she looked at what you could become and believed you into being. We've seen examples of this in the people we've identified as valuing us — those who've treated us with unconditional dignity.

Think back to Dr. Ben Carson's mom, Sonya. She saw little Ben "telescopically." She saw his potential and strengths, not his faults and weaknesses.

When we see people microscopically, we look at their foibles and weaknesses, instead of examining their assets and building upon them. We highlight their flaws and tear them apart.

When people do this, it is not because they are *evil* as much as *insecure*. We wrongly believe we will be stronger if others are weaker — as if there is only so much potential to go around.

In fact, the opposite is true. The more you see people telescopically, the more "telescopic people" will be drawn to you (people who will look for your potential and dignity). The old adage is true, "Like calls to like..."

Daniel Goleman is an author and psychologist who has written ten books including the best-sellers, Emotional Intelligence (1998, Bantam Books) and Social Intelligence; The New Science of Human Relationships (2006, Bantam Books). Goleman is largely responsible for making popular the science of emotional intelligence and emotional quotient (EQ). This field focuses on enhancing human potential by building compassion.

Your EQ is similar to your ability to see people telescopically, to empathize with others and call out their strengths.

While IQ is largely stable from childhood, your EQ — Emotional Quotient — has nearly limitless potential for growth. EQ is the combination of multiple skills

- The ability to *motivate yourself*
- The ability to *motivate others*
- The ability to *empathize*
- The ability to *influence*

What's more, EQ is an acquired skill (which means it can be grown), while IQ is largely an innate ability, set from childhood.

You can grow EQ through a variety of exercises.

- Allowing yourself to develop, not repress, your emotions
- Choosing to give others the BOD (Benefit Of the Doubt); seeing other people telescopically, not microscopically
- Intentionally building time in your day to learn about others
- Building the habit of giving others specific compliments based upon observing their behavior

Goleman cites research that indicates your EQ is far more related to better relationships, increased success and a higher quality of living than IQ. Yet, we often focus on increasing a person's IQ by 1-2% over a lifetime as opposed to exponentially increasing an individual's EQ.

In similar research, neuroeconomist and professor at Claremont Graduate University, Paul Zak, pioneered the field of Moral Markets. His extensive research indicates the strongest economies are found in nations of high trust (Moral Markets: The Critical Role of Values in the Economy, Princeton University Press, 2008). As trust weakens in a nation — so does its economy.

Zak has even been able to link trust to the release of a single chemical in the body, Oxytocin. He calls it "The Moral Molecule."

When the body releases oxytocin, it creates emotions of acceptance and trust. Ninety-six percent of the population can release the hormone, but — like a muscle — you can "lose it if you don't use it."

When the body releases oxytocin, it creates emotions of acceptance and trust

Children raised in low trust environments can experience a diminished capacity to release oxytocin. However, that capacity can be restored!

You've experienced the effect of oxytocin if you've had goose bumps or felt near tears over a moving song, movie, hearing a compassionate story or witnessing someone being kind to another person.

You can grow the ability to release this molecule in ways similar to growing your EQ. Collect acts of compassion — videos clips, stories, songs, art or go out of your way to be compassionate to someone in need.

This is why, in the schools and businesses I consult, we focus on building trust through simple acts of intentional courtesy. Why the focus on courtesy? Because focusing on bullying actually increases bullying. Even seeing the phrase, "Do not bully," releases pleasurable endorphins in children who've had positive experiences with such behavior.

Plus, no one hears, "*Not*."

If I wrote, "Do *not* think of hot fudge sundaes." What does your mind turn to? Before you can *not* think of something, you must *first* think about it.

Courtesy builds trust and trust helps us learn. When we are afraid, we cannot think creatively. Fear shuts down higher order learning. We can memorize — just as an alligator can memorize (imprint) situations where it must "fight or take flight." But our "alligator brains" cannot create.

I share with educators, "As soon as you say, 'This is going to be on the test,' you might as well be teaching the chair because the student has stopped learning and begun memorizing — They will forget what you teach them."

Instead, we can invite students to play or apply their new-found knowledge by asking, "How can you see this information fitting into your life? How can you apply it today?"

Courtesy is not just the building block of EQ (and a strong causal action for the release of oxytocin) it is also the core foundation of building relationships and communities. Sustained acts of simple courtesy can reignite a dying relationship. Remember what we said earlier in Chapter 1; "When courtesy thrives, relationships thrive, communities thrive. When courtesy dies, so do our relationships and our communities."

I learned this lesson from a young man named, Maclean. He was a Grade 11 student at a high school in British Columbia and I was speaking to his grade about social equality. Shortly before I spoke in that city, a local boy had been hospitalized as a result of bullying. The horrific act occurred within a block of the school property.

Taking the article with me, I taped it to the wall, asked the students to read it and then inquired, "It doesn't make sense to me to talk about equality in the world, when a child was beat up within minutes of this school. What can we do about *that* issue?"

With amazing candor, Maclean stood to his feet in front of 200 peers and said, "Mr. Jerry, I'm going to find that bus stop, find that kid and be his friend."

With a simple, succinct statement, Maclean captured the most influential course of action that could be taken. While most adults might respond with statements like, "We need more cops patrolling this area," "We need more security cameras," or, "We need to teach more anti-bullying courses in our schools," Maclean's response, "I'm going to find that bus stop, find that kid and be his friend," aimed at the *source of the opportunity* — not the *result of the problem:* Honor the dignity of those least accepted and most rejected.

"I'm going to find that bus stop, find that kid and be his friend," aimed at the *source of the opportunity* — not the *result of the problem.*

That action required no authority and no resources. By the end of the day, Maclean and his classmates had mapped out all the bus stops within a square kilometer of their school and worked out a system so 2-3 students could be at each stop from 3:00 p.m. to 3:30 p.m. daily (the most dangerous time to be a child in North America).

Without knowing, Maclean had 1) stated a compassionate focus and 2) built a community around his vision.

Maclean saw the problem as an opportunity. He responded telescopically and influentially. His short statement, "Find the bus stop, find the kid, be his friend," was so elegant and succinct that it drew an emotional response (oxytocin release) from his own classmates — and they changed their world. They *replaced bullying,* by *increasing courtesy.*

Raising your EQ is your direct link to moving others on a molecular level. Like Maclean, the greatest habit you can grow is to become an influential person by listening telescopically to others and seeing how your compassionate foci can complement each other. Examine the challenges around you and seek influential, simple sources of opportunity.

3. Your Personality Strengths

The best methods of identifying your own personality strengths are by talking to those who value you or by taking an online personality assessment. The two I prefer are "Strengthfinders 2.0 (Gallup Press, 2007)" — to find out about your strengths — and "Emotional Intelligence 2.0 (Talent Smart, 2009)" — to find out how to grow your EQ.

You can find these books at most bookstores or order them online. In the back of each book is a code that will allow you take an online assessment and print out a personalized report.

Tom Rath (who wrote Strengthfinders 2.0 and Strengths Based Leadership) writes that extensive research at the Gallup Organization reveals four major personality domains and 34 strengths within those domains. The themes are:

1. Executing: Prone towards action, enjoys taking steps to initiate new projects or solve existing problems.

2. Strategic: Prone towards planning. Enjoys gathering all the facts and looking at all the possibilities before initiating activity or moving to resolve any issues.

3. Influence: Prone towards inspiring, enjoys sharing ideas with others, motivating and convincing them to consider a certain action. Will motivate people to see past a problem or, instead, look for the opportunities.

4. Relational: Prone towards empathy. Enjoys learning about people and sharing with them on a deep level. In stress, they want to find out how people are feeling.

There are multiple combinations of strengths under each theme and the odds of ever meeting someone who has the same strengths in the same order as you are 1 in 33 million. Generally, a person might have a few strengths in different themes, but one theme will be dominant.

Surely all the strengths have blind sides — strategists might spend too much time planning, executors may lean towards a "ready, fire, aim," approach to life, influencers may network with a lot of people but no one deeply, relational people may get stuck examining feelings. The beauty of a strengths-based approach is it helps people know the areas of their life where they will thrive (eustress) and the areas of their life that will cause them distress.

Knowing your own personal strengths will also help you understand that every person has a distinct way of viewing life and that even how we trust is relevant to our strengths.

Someone high in relationship strengths will build trust in deep conversations, whereas a person high in execution strengths would generally rather act on issues than talk about them. Who is right? Of course, *neither* is right and *both* are right — from their personal viewpoint.

Yet, in order to build trust with others we have to be able to recognize our strengths and build on theirs.

In order to build trust with others we have to be able to recognize our strengths and build on theirs.

In addition, strengths are not skills. You might be a wonderful motivator, influencing people and crowds around you and yet not have any Influencer Strengths. Indeed, all of us must act at times outside of our strength themes. However, if you aren't an influencer and must spend a great deal of time influencing others it could drain your energy and cause distress you will later need to deal with in a positive way.

Knowing your strengths allows you to plan ahead for times you will be operating outside your comfort zone and gives you the opportunity to build in "down times" after those endeavors.

See Exercise 3.1a or 3.1b to identify your unique personality strengths.

Q3: Mastery

The third component of your Compassionate Focus is mastery, what talents and skills you want to master. Your strengths will tell you about your personality and your EQ will tell you how to improve your interpersonal relationships. Your talents and skills will assist you in how best to work with your personality in a way that will motivate yourself and others to affect the causes you identified in the first quadrant.

We often pigeonhole people in certain careers or steer them in directions based upon their IQ, rather than their drive, strengths and skills.

For example, a young adult might tell a guidance counselor, "My grandmother died of cancer and I want to do something about that disease."

A rushed or disengaged counselor might look up the student's marks and say, "Well, your science and math scores show very little proficiency. You should consider another career."

There are a couple important truths we miss when we think that way.

Instead of building a career, most people will be building *resumes.*

First, our lives are rapidly moving out of a career-based economy. It will be increasingly hard to find lifelong "careers" in a single occupation in this fast paced environment. Instead of building a *career*, most people will be building *resumes* and the fastest growing sector of the economy will be in entrepreneurial areas — people who start their own small businesses. In particular, the fastest growth will take place in social entrepreneurialism — people who start businesses based upon a cause, offering pragmatic solutions to complex social issues.

Just think, by the end of this guide, you will have all the tools you need to start your social entrepreneurial opportunity!

Secondly, having high marks in a certain field of study doesn't mean you will 1) enjoy doing it, 2) make a good living at it, or 3) even stay with it for very long. Sadly, too many people find out this truth late in their lives and then feel stuck in jobs they hate.

If you know what you are passionate about and how to build a network of support around that passion, whatever you do will not only be successful, but meaningful as well.

For example, what if a young man was passionate about cancer and wanted to influence people, yet he was mostly great at athletics? Should he give up doing something significant about cancer?

Consider the life of the young Terry Fox (July 28, 1958 – June 28, 1981). Terry's right leg was amputated in 1977 due to cancer. Despite this, he decided to run cross-Canada to raise money for cancer research.

Terry ran an equivalent of a marathon a day until cancer forced him to end his quest. Despite the disease, he ran 143 days and completed 5,373 kilometres (3,339 miles).

The "Terry Fox Run," started in his honor, has since raised over C$500 million and remains the largest single-day fund-raiser in Canadian history.

School marks can be an indicator of talents and skills but they are not the only one. Combined with your passion and strengths, whatever you're talented at doing (art, communication, music, math, cooking, science, technology, or writing — just to name a few areas) will create an unstoppable force when fused with a network of supportive people.

Take the time now to list what talents and skills you want to master.

See Activity 3.2

Q4: Networking, Who will support you in pursuing your focus?

We've stated a number of times the primary purpose of this guidebook is to help you identify your compassionate focus and build a network of people around your direction.

All along you've been building a team of people who value you and are now helping you develop this important roadmap. Now, it is time to start expanding your network to include a greater number of people committed to your meaningful life and the causes that move you.

Remember some important statements we've already discussed about building your network:

- People who value you unconditionally believe in your dignity, this is different than people who offer "performance-based approval (giving their approval when you do what they want you to do)."
- People who value you will want you to expand your network, instead of trying to isolate you from those who care about you.
- The more influential you are, the more you will plan your week by who you need to see instead of just *what* you need to *do*.
- To create a meaningful life, you have to create your own plan for life-long learning. This includes identifying people who will mentor you.

Now, we're going to do an activity that will help you build your network of support.

See Activity 3.3

Develop your own powerful social profile

Juan was incarcerated in a detention center in Washington State that was using one of my programs. He was 16 and deeply involved in local gangs. John was his mentor, in his 70's, a retired Army Accountant. Except for their names, they couldn't have been more different.

Yet, John valued Juan's dignity and agreed to mentor him through our Significant Conversations program.

On that particular Tuesday, we were studying "networking your way out of poverty," and the topic was a theory called "Six Degrees of Separation."

This concept states we are never more than six relationships away from reaching anyone in the world whom we desire to meet.

Juan responded, "I question that paradigm (of course his statement was slightly more colorful than what I just said...)."

"Really," I queried, "Let's try it out, who would you like to reach, Juan?"

He pointed to a book on the wall, Always Running: La Vida Loca; Gang Days in L.A. (1995, Scholarly Books), by Entrepreneur, Luis J. Rodriquez. The book was about how Mr. Rodriquez worked his way out of gangs by starting a series of LA-Based coffeehouses with Latino themes, poetry and art.

Currently, Mr. Rodriquez helps others break the cycle of gangs by hiring them and training them in his coffeehouses.

I had Juan and John work on two simple tasks.

1. Write to Mr. Rodriquez, tell him where you are, where you'd like to be, and ask for his help.

2. Find a way to get your letter to Mr. Rodriquez.

They finished the letter in about twenty minutes and read it aloud to the group. Then we asked, "How will you get that letter to the author?"

Suggestions were to mail it regular postal service or to e-mail it. Juan didn't have the Author's e-mail address or access to the Internet. However, on the back of the book was the Publishers web site (One degree of separation) and his mentor, John, had access to the Internet (Two degrees of separation).

Juan asked John to e-mail the note and John heartily agreed.

Within *not* two months, *not* two weeks, *not* two days, but two *hours*, John received an e-mail from Mr. Rodriquez with a six point plan for breaking the cycle of gang behavior in his life (Three degrees of separation).

John immediately contacted me and asked if he had to wait until the next week's program to share the letter with Juan. I replied, "John, if you don't beat me to the detention center I'm stealing your thunder."

Of course, John beat me there. Juan was stunned and after composing a thank you letter, the two of them used the correspondence from Mr. Rodriquez to lead the following week's class.

Three degrees, not even six.

Today, we live in an Internet society and people like author, Mitch Joel, say there are no longer, "Six Degrees of Separation," but, "Six Pixels of Separation (Six Pixels of Separation; Everyone's Connected, 2012, Grand Central Publishing)."

With a positive social profile, you can reach almost anyone nearly instantaneously. You just have to have a compelling enough invitation (we'll be working on that in a later chapter).

Right now, we're going to use your Compassionate Focus and Values Statements, plus the media that you've been collecting to tell people how amazing you are! How you are enchanting, engaging, encouraging and enthusiastic.

To build a powerful social profile, remember these 7 key Internet commandments.

INTERNET COMMANDMENTS

1. Whatever you say on the Internet is there for everyone and forever. Employers can look it up, people you respect, prospective clients — everything you say is for everyone and forever.

2. Never attack people; you can respectfully disagree with people's positions, but don't attack people's character.

3. Be solution based. Don't just come up with what is wrong with the world, talk about potential actions to resolve issues. Bring people to your network that are looking to make the world better.

4. Be positive, steer away from sarcasm and cynicism, the twin diseases of powerlessness.

5. Always have trusted and honest people with whom you can discuss your ideas before saying anything important or controversial.

6. Use positive media to accent your points (ARTiculate your viewpoint).

7. A real key to remember is that we no longer live in a Competitive Economy. The Internet is a Trust Economy. Build trust with your readers and they'll send their friends and help you grow. Never say or do anything that would lose the trust of your supporters.

See Activity 3.4

Activity 3.1a: Identifying your strengths, Online Assessment

If you are able to take an online assessment, take the following steps

- Step 1: If you have to choose between the Strengthfinders Assessment and Emotional Intelligence, I would begin with Strengthfinders. Purchase the book, locate your assessment code and learn your top five strengths.
- Step 2: Repeat for Emotional Intelligence 2.0 if you are able. Print your assessment(s) and read them thoroughly. Underline the segments of your assessments that intrigue you.
- Step 3: Create a note and begin by listing your Strengthfinders Results and what interested you under each strength area.
- Step 4: Share your results with at least three people who value you. Ask for their input. Write down things they said that were significant to you.

STRENGTH	WHAT INTERESTED ME	WHAT INTERESTED OTHERS
Example: Strategic	*I almost always like to think things through before I act.*	*They said this fits me like a glove and see how it has helped my decisions.*

STRENGTH	WHAT INTERESTED ME	WHAT INTERESTED OTHERS

Activity 3.1b: Identifying your strengths, Personal Assessment

If you are unable to take the online assessment, take the following steps.

- Step 1: Examine the four themes of the Strengths, make a note here and write down the name of the strength. Next to the strength, write a numeric weight for that strength. Choose from 0 – 10 depending on how strong you think each theme describes you (0 is "doesn't match me at all," 10 is "matches me completely"). When added together, the sum of all four should not be greater than 10. Explain why you think each strength fits or doesn't fit your personality.
- Step 2: Share the themes with at least three people who value you. Ask them to rate your strengths as well and see how closely they match your personal assessment.
- Step 3: Write down your results and observations in your notes.

Example (Author's Strength Themes)

Strength Theme	Weight	Explanation
Executing	3	*This isn't my top strength, but once I make a plan, I act on it*
Strategic	5	*This is my greatest strength, I like to collect information, weigh options, make a solid plan of action and then get it done.*
Influence	0	*I am good at motivating people but it is stressful for me. It is a skill I have, but not something I enjoy.*
Relationship	2	*I like to understand what people are thinking, I also enjoy helping people feel like they can be part of a team to reach common goals or address common issues.*

Your Themes

Strength Theme	Weight	Explanation
Executing		
Strategic		
Influence		
Relationship		

Activity 3.2:
Identifying your talents and skills

Step 1: Skills I want to Master:

Make a list of areas where you have distinct talents and skills. What are you really great at doing? Consider areas of study you enjoy or understand easily. Write down hobbies that interest you enough to grow and become masterful at them.

Step 2: What Others See

Share the above list with three people you know and respect. Ask for their input and write a summary of responses in your note.

Step 3: Life Possibilities

Ask someone with a career or guidance counseling background to show you books and/or articles steering you towards professions in areas of your passions and talents. Ask how starting a business or working with a company in those areas might fit with your personality strengths. Include their responses in your note.

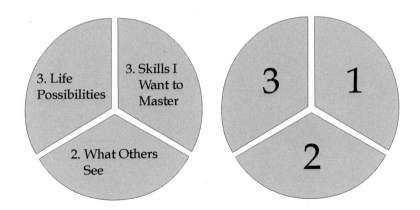

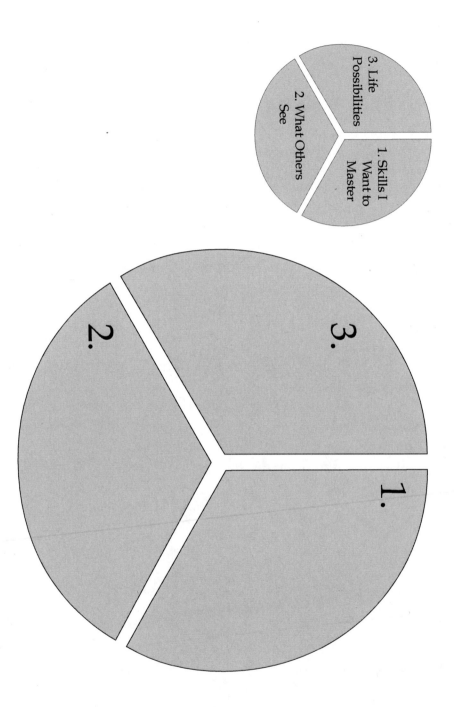

Activity 3.3:
Build Your Supportive Network

STEP 1: COMPASSIONATE SUPPORTERS

Make a note listing 3 people who inspire you or are already working on a cause that moves you. List not only people you know, but people in your area of interest who live locally or globally.

Review this list and put a note by those names identifying whom you would like to connect with This Week, This Month, or within Three Months.

BUILD YOUR OWN NETWORK: COMPASSION

List three people that inspire you because of their work on a cause that moves you. Include people who work in your area of interest either locally or globally. Write out their name, their cause and when you'd like to meet them. Later, we'll create a strategy for connecting with them.

Example

Name: Sir Ken Robinson

Cause: Create a more engaging and entrepreneurial education system

Date: February 28, 2013

Name: _____

Cause: _____

_____

_____

Date: _____

Name: _____

Cause: _____

_____

_____

Date: _____

Name: _____

Cause: _____

_____

_____

Date: _____

Name: _____

Cause: _____

_____

_____

Date: _____

STEP 2: STRENGTH SUPPORTERS

Build a team of at least 3 people with whom you can regularly connect who are strongest in areas that might be your blind spots. For example, if you are high in relationship, but low in strategy, find someone who is high in strategy and who can help you create new strategies for improving your life.

In his book, Strength Based Leadership (Gallup Press, 2009), author Tom Rath recalled his grandfather, Donald Clifton, being asked if — after 40 years of strength-based leadership research — had he found any typology of a great leader?

Clifton's responded there was no evidence of a specific strength set that made one a great leader, but that great leaders lead from their strengths and build teams around their weaknesses."

STRENGTH – COACHES: MAKE YOUR OWN MENTORS

Make a note of at least 1 person who looks at situations from a different perspective than you based upon their strengths. Place their names under the following categories:

1. Executing

When I am frozen by inaction, who will help me get moving?

NAME:_____

2. Strategy

Who will help me create a good plan?

NAME:_____

3. Relational

Who will help me develop my empathy and inclusiveness/ communication skills?

NAME: _____

4. Influence

Who can help me share my ideas and motivate others?

NAME: _____

STEP 3: MASTERY COACHES

Review the talents and your skills you want to master. List at least 3 people that can help you improve them? Who can connect you with someone that can be a mentor, coach, instructor or teacher in your particular area of skill? Who already makes a living from what you'd like to do.

Name:_____ Skill: _____

Name:_____ Skill: _____

Name:_____ Skill: _____

Activity 3.4: ARTiculate your Own compassionate focus

Use the following form to begin creating your own compassionate focus. To make it even more powerful, create a poster-sized collage ARTiculating your focus. Use art, media, and quotes to fill in each area. Review the activities you've done in this chapter to add your own flair to the collage.

Done well, this will be something that you keep near you to motivate you as you grow. It will also become a root part of your own personal web site and compelling invitation (the invitation you will use to draw others to your cause).

In the following areas, include a collage of items as described:

INSPIRING CAUSES

- A short definition of your top inspiring causes.
- Art, quotes and media that will frequently inspire you to pursue this cause.

PERSONALITY STRENGTHS

- List your unique personality strengths and a short summary of their definitions.
- Art, quotes and media that remind you of your strengths and people who might have strengths similar to you.

TALENTS AND SKILLS

- List the talents and skills you want to master.
- Art, quotes and media that accent your talents and skills.

SUPPORTERS

- List the people who can support you in order of when you will connect with them.
- If you have articles, quotes, pictures, logos, or web sites, related to these people, put them in this section as well.

VALUES STATEMENT

- In the center of the poster, put a copy of your Values Statement business card.

MY COMPASSIONATE FOCUS

What are your unique
personality strengths?

What moves you? Who in-
spires you?

Your
Values
Statement

What skills or talents do you
want to master?

Who will support your
comassionate focus?

Activity 3.5:
Build your positive social profile

There are multiple Social Profile web sites on the Internet and most of them have pre-set questions you answer about yourself. What we'll be doing is creating the components for your own web site. You can (and probably would like to) use other social profile tools (like Facebook) to link people to your own web site and blogs.

Actually creating your own web site can be done at a later time using a template on an Internet service site or by hiring someone who has experience in this area (they'll love you because you will already have so many of the components completed). You might consider going to a local college or university and seeing if any of the students want to do your site for credit and a lower fee.

Here are components to consider on your site:

Home Page

- Your name and contact information (e-mail).
- Your values statement and a general summary of your compassionate focus.
- Two or three pictures that accent your values statement and focus. One can be of you if you feel it will accent your point. Use a logo if you have developed one.
- Keep this information brief; a person should be able to read this page in less than twenty seconds.

More than anything, this page should immediately build trust with your viewers and make them want to interact with your site. Remember when we talked about Oxytocin? This page should help your audience connect with you and release oxytocin.

Interactive Headings

Here are some suggestions for your interactive headings. These go across the top of the web page and link to further content.

About Me | Causes That Inspire Me | Gifts and Talents | Support Page | Media and Blogs

Causes That Inspire Me

This is information from Section 1 of your Compassionate Focus.

- List your top causes and use media to accent your points.
- In each section, the simpler the better, people can always read more in your blog / media section.

Every section should have an opportunity for the viewer to interact with you or get involved.

About Me

This is from Section 2 of you Compassionate Focus. Here you can go further into your values and strengths.

- Share about your accomplishments to date in working towards your causes.

Gifts and Talents

This is information from Section 3 of your Compassionate Focus. Use this for two purposes, 1) How you can assist them through the use of your gifts and talents. 2) How others can become involved in your cause.

Support Page

Ask the people you've connecting with in Section 4 to share testimonials; positive things people have said about you.

Blogs and Media

Here is where you can inspire people and share your ideas more fully.

- Include plenty of media here. Links to videos, summaries of books, songs, or other art forms that people will find inspiring. Keep in mind copyright laws, you can link to other people's media, but not make copies or give away copies of copyrighted material. It is not only illegal, but unethical. This is how many people make a living or provide an income for others.
- Talk about people or groups doing positive things.
- This is the section where you want people to continually return and refer others. Make it exciting, engaging, become a center of information in your area. Build trust, release oxytocin and help people get involved.
- Again, remember to give people simple ways they can be involved.

Continually keep in mind how you can build trust with your readers. How can they trust your content? How can they feel more inspired? Who will you motivate them to make a difference?

IV
Commitments

Define YOUR Commitments
Choose to Excel

Defining your long-term commitments is critical to living a compassionate life. Commitments are promises you make to yourself. They are destinations you challenge yourself to reach as you journey towards your compassionate focus. If we are to find meaning in life, it is important to trade some of our short-term desires for long-term commitments.

MAKE A COMMITMENT

Dara Torres is a record-breaker. An Olympic athlete, she broke many records in swimming, winning multiple medals. When Dara attended her first Olympics, it was 1984; she was 15 years old and set the world record in the 50-meter freestyle.

At that time, most "experts" thought female swimmers peaked in their teens and their bodies couldn't endure the training necessary for such an intense sport.

Dara also medaled at the 1988 Olympics and the 1992 Olympics. Then, at the age of 33, the oldest member of the US Olympic Swim Team, she medaled yet again at the 2000 Olympics.

Quite an impressive record-breaker!

By the way, at age 40, 15 months after giving birth to her first child, Ms. Torres medaled at the 2008 Olympics, where she broke her own American record for the 50-meter freestyle! The same record she had set at 15.

The same record she had set at 15

In addition to her swimming records, Dara is a model, an inspirational speaker and an author of two books, Age Is Just A Number (Broad Way Books, 2009) and Gold Medal Fitness (Crown Publishing, 2010).

Dara doesn't train only when she feels like it. She's up before dawn, five days a week working with weights, stretching, and — of course — in the water. Her coach, Mark Schubert, once said of her, "I don't think she's ever been out of shape a day in her life. I think that's what makes this possible and conceivable."

Dara has made multiple commitments in her life. Swimming is only one. She's committed to being a mom, and gives her time to fund-raise for multiple charitable organizations. She is committed to her work as an author and speaker. In every situation, when Dara makes a commitment you can rely on her to keep it.

A commitment — like a value — is a choice you make and keep regardless of your circumstances, peer approval or when it is convenient. Commitments link your Compassionate Focus to what is best for your life in the long-term.

A commitment — like a value — is a choice you make and keep regardless of your circumstances, peer approval or when it is convenient.

For now, let's look at that phrase, "long-term." Essential to living a meaningful life is the concept of "delayed gratification"; being able to put off short-term pleasure and/or endure short-term discomfort in exchange for long-term gain.

Imagine people like Dana who seek to be Olympic athletes, can they practice only when they feel like it, when the water is warm or it is sunny outside? How about someone who wants to start a new business? Can she focus on her business or put money into her enterprise only when she is in the right mood?

Consider an individual who is passionate about finding a cure for cancer or resolving water poverty in our world? Would that person have to give up some short-term pleasures for long-term gains? Do you think they might run into opposition from people who said their dreams were crazy or wanted them to forget studying and go to a party instead?

Certainly people like Dara do spontaneous things too. We have to be open to the moment and enjoy the day as it unfolds. What we seek is a balance, not a regimen. Seek the joy of the moment, but when you make a commitment, stick to them, "No matter what."

See Activity 4.1, Commitment Discussions

Commitments and Checkpoints

Hannah Taylor is considered one of the 100 most powerful women in Canada, quite a feat for someone who is still in her teens. She tells her audience, "When I was five years old, I saw a wrong for the first time..."

She witnessed a man digging through a dumpster for food and bottles, something she felt no one should have to do in order to live. In response, Hannah started the Ladybug Foundation to take on the challenge of homelessness and poverty in Canada. To date, her organization has raised over two million dollars and is involved in supporting over 50 homeless shelters across Canada.

Hannah's commitment to her cause is amazing and unfaltering. Her values statement is simple and straightforward.

Hannah's Values Statement:

"I believe that if people know about homelessness – that there are people living without a home – they will want to help."

Hannah's Commitments:

Hannah's values spill over into her commitments.

1. To teach people that people who are homeless are just like you and me. They just need us to love them and care for them.

2. To teach everyone to treat people who are homeless like family because if you do that you will love them in all the right ways and you will treat them in all the right ways and care for them in all the rights ways.

3. To teach people that no one should ever eat from a garbage can or live without a bed or a home and let them know that there are people that have to because they have no choice.

4. To ask every person who will listen to help however they can to make life for people who are homeless better.

5. To teach people that everyone can make a difference in the lives of others.

ALL OF THIS INFORMATION CAN BE FOUND ON THE LADYBUG FOUNDATION'S WEBSITE: WWW.LADYBUGFOUNDATION.CA

You can see Hannah has made many commitments, especially in the areas of how she teaches and treats people. She has made a commitment to teaching people about the underlying truths of homelessness and also committed to treat all people like they are part of her family.

Commitments are long-term ideals driving your direction and deepening your Compassionate Focus. They may not be something you actually achieve, but they continually motivate you.

Commitments are long-term ideals driving your direction and deepening your Compassionate Focus. They may not be something you actually achieve, but they continually motivate you.

For example, a relational commitment might be, "I am a master communicator, skilled at motivating people to achieve their optimal performance in life."

Don't worry about filling in all the commitments at once. Keep in mind the Five Percent Principle we discussed earlier. Take on one area of your life at a time, otherwise you might feel overwhelmed.

Ask yourself, "What commitment will I make today that will move me five percent closer to my Compassionate Focus?"

Start with one commitment you want to make in your life, create a compelling statement about that commitment and then develop some checkpoints to help you identify when you are moving in the right direction. Once you've completed that step, the sense of accomplishment will give you more motivation to make other commitments in your life.

SEVEN AREAS OF BALANCE

Burnout is not the result of doing *too many* things. It is the result of doing *the same thing* too many times.

Burnout is not the result of doing *too many* things. It is the result of doing *the same thing* too many times.

People who sustain their vision over years are focused and may even seem intense. If you remember the Four E's we looked at in Chapter 1, we would say they are enthused (en-theos), burning with a passionate fire — even zeal.

Individuals who maintain a healthy focus in life balance their passionate endeavors with healthy physical habits, deep relationships, and joyful re-creation. Without these counter-weights, they become unbalanced and unhealthy. Eventually, this results in burnout; depression, a sense of isolation, focusing on results without respect for the people who are working towards them, ends without meaning and outcomes without values.

This is why some of the most brilliant people in the world often lose their joy or even — in some cases — their moral balance.

Richard Nixon is a primary example. Political historians have cited his foreign policy — and especially his work with China — as among the best of all US presidents. Sadly, he will be mostly remembered as the first US president to ever be impeached.

His undoing was his paranoiac focus on power and surrounding

BALANCE QUOTES

"Prosperity is not just scale, adversity is the only balance to weigh friends
— Plutarch, 46-119

"The most important human endeavor is the striving for morality in our actions. Our inner balance and even our very existence depend on it. Only morality in our actions can give beauty and dignity to life."
— Albert Einstein, 1879-1955

"Work, love and play are the greatest balance wheels of man's being."
— Orison Swett Marden, 1850-1924

"Happiness is not a matter of intensity, but of balance, order, rhythm and harmony.
— Thomas Merton, 1915-1968

"A well-developed sense of humor is the pole that adds balance to your step as you walk the tightrope of life."
— William Arthur Ward, 1921-1994

himself with people who fed his delusions instead of challenging them.

He was a man without balance, focused on a solitary goal — political power — with no counterweight to his pursuits and no true friends to be honest with him.

The seven areas of balance are designed to prevent you from burning out or losing your moral compass. They look at multiple facets in your life, not just one area.

1. Educational Commitments: Lifelong learning goals for continual personal improvement.

2. Financial Commitments: Pursuing financial independence by balancing needs, wants and income.

3. Physical Commitments: A healthy energized life balancing diet, sleep and exercise.

4. Professional Commitments: Articulating your compassionate focus, building a community of support around it and including how you will support your vision financially.

5. Recreational Commitments: Bringing joy to your life through volunteering, hobbies, activities or the arts. Think of these commitments as ways to re-create yourself.

6. Relational Commitments: Identifying how you will treat others and how you want to be treated. Also, identifying specific relationships in your life you want to deepen or develop.

7. Spiritual Commitments: How will you increase your sense of meaning, purpose and compassion?

See Activity 4.2 Seven Areas of Balance

Continue to share your values statement, compassionate focus and now, your commitments, with people who inspire you. Ask those who value you to occasionally query you about whether you are aligning your life with your checkpoints.

Here are your three greatest tools for fulfilling your commitments.

1. You wrote them down.

2. You shared them with people who value you.

3. You check your progress regularly.

As you reflect on Dara and Hannah. Consider ways their commitments have served them in their lives. How have they articulated and lived out their commitments? How has each one built a supportive network around her focus? What type of support did they need to attain their commitments and how did they develop that support?

As you examine these questions, think of ways you can examine their behaviors as a model to guide you. Consider how you can use their example to increase the direction and influence in your life.

Become the person you want to be by learning the behaviors of the people you admire.

Commitment to Action

ACTION STEPS

Your Values Statement and Compassionate Focus will rarely change. Your commitments might deepen over time as you grow, but what will constantly change are the Action Steps or Tasks you accomplish to move closer to your commitments.

An Action Step is a short-term task that has two core components:

1. An Action Step is attached to a timeline.

2. Upon completion, you can mark it off as done.

For high effectiveness, Action Steps must also follow the 3P's we've highlighted earlier. Think of it like this, "To have Infinite Power ($P\infty$), your Action Steps must have 3P's." $P\infty = P1 \times P2 \times P3$.

P1 Positive

Use only positive sentences that focus you on what you will do — not what you won't do. For example, "I will keep carrot and celery sticks in my fridge," is much more positive than, "I won't eat potato chips."

P2 Present-Tense

Keep your Action Steps in the present reality, not centered on a future possibility. "I do 50 pushups every morning when I awake," is much more present tense then, "I'll get in shape some day."

P3 Precise:

Precise means you know exactly what you are setting out to accomplish, your tasks are not wishy-washy or subjective. "I run forty minutes on Monday, Wednesday and Friday at 1200," is much more precise than, "I should run sometime this week."

Here is an illustration to keep in mind as you consider why the 3P's give you power. Imagine stepping into a taxicab in New York City and telling the cabbie, "I *don't* want to go to Manhattan."

How do you think that cabbie is going to respond?

Telling yourself what not to do is like telling a cabbie where you don't want to go. You won't get where you're going if you don't define how you're going to get there.

Telling yourself what not to do is like telling a cabbie where you don't want to go. You won't get where you're going if you don't define how you're going to get there.

Cop-Out Words

One young man told me he wanted to be reliable so he could receive a good reference from his current job. He had mentioned how he had a hard time waking up and getting to work on time in the past.

"So," I inquired, "Does that mean you're ready to get to sleep earlier on Sunday if you're working on Monday morning?"

"I'll *really* try," he replied.

"So you won't then?" I responded.

"What?" he said somewhat defensively. "I just said 'I'd *really* try.'"

Looking at him with complete sincerity, I asked, "Michael, if I were your pilot and you asked me to fly you to Toronto. Would you be more likely to fly with me if I said, 'Absolutely!' or, 'I'll *really* try.'"

Michael looked at me for a long time. Then he said, "I see what you mean Mr. G. I guess I'm not being honest with myself... or you."

"Now you are, Michael," I said.

Though Michael and I had a caring conversation, I can honestly say, I wasn't much help to him. It is impossible to help a bird fly if he won't flap his own wings. It was like pouring water in a glass with no bottom. I could continue to invest in Michael — and would have — but he had to invest in himself as well.

The quickest way to tell if someone is choosing to grow is if that person is willing to *divest* his or her life of cop-out words and willing to *invest* in real commitments.

The quickest way to tell if someone is choosing to grow is if that person is willing to divest his or her life of cop-out words and willing to invest in real commitments.

Cop-out words build excuses to my failures. I'll really *try*. I would if I *could*. I *might* be able to do that. *If* I can. I *wish*, I *hope*, we'll see...

Other cop-out phrases begin with the word, "Well," or "Yeah but..."

"Well, I'd try that but..."

"Yeah but, I don't have this or that..."

These words and phrases increase a "Victim Mentality" in our life — a focus on what we don't have, or can't do.

I had to respect Michael when he said, "I see what you mean Mr. G. I guess I'm not being honest with myself... or you."

When our "yes," is "yes," and our "no," is "no," we have begun to make a commitment to ourselves. We're no longer fooling ourselves with non-committal statements.

As you develop your Action Steps and Commitments, examine your own language to make sure it doesn't include terms that undermine your intent from the start. There is no greater distraction in your life than to waste time over what we might do or possibly try. Your life is too important and time too valuable to waste your breath on cop-outs.

See Activity 4.3 Strike Out The Cop-Out Words

Motivation:
The Value and Efficacy Equation

THE EFFICACY FACTOR

Efficacy is a wonderful word. It combines two concepts into one term.

- Want: I *want* to pursue this commitment — desire and value.
- Will: I *will* be able to pursue this commitment — expectation and effectiveness.

If your efficacy is negative your motivation will be negative. In order for your motivation to be high, your *want* and *will* must be high. If either variable is negative, your motivation will be negative.

Consider my work in juvenile centers. If I asked a group of young people, "How many of you *want* to come back to juvie?"

The result would usually be zero. Most everyone in the juvenile detention center would rather be some place else.

If I asked, "How many of you *expect* to come back here?"

Nearly everyone in the room would raise their hand. I obviously didn't have to deal with a *want* problem. I had to deal with a *will* problem. The young people didn't want to come back, but they expected they would.

Arresting people takes them out of their situation but it doesn't change their circumstances. In most cases, the young person will return to the same home, the same neighborhood, just with an additional set of problems. They now have court fees and fines that must be paid and community time that must be served. They will have regular meetings with a probation officer who is overloaded and really can't spend the one-on-one time needed to find out how the young person is truly doing.

At some point, living the life of a contributing citizen becomes demotivating compared to going back to life a life of criminal behavior. Unless the expectation is changed, the desire alone won't sustain the motivation to stay out.

In order to remain highly motivated to pursue your commitments, you must incorporate the Efficacy Factor. You must have both the want and the will to pursue your goals.

1. Do I *want* this? Yes or no — no cop-out words.

2. *Will* I be able to make progress toward this goal? Yes or no — no cop-out words.

You can even rate your responses on a scale from negative 10 to positive 10. Keeping in mind that if either your will or want is negative; you will lose the motivation to pursue your commitment.

THE EFFECTIVENESS ISSUE

Most people lose their motivation on the will side (effectiveness), not the want side (desire). For example, I've met people who had a high desire to lose weight or complete a degree program or improve their relationships; they just didn't have positive expectations. It wasn't the desire that undermined their motivation — it was their expectation.

In fact, the higher your desire and the lower your expectation the more your motivation will be negative (the opposite it true as well.

You can change your expectation by making your action steps more achievable. Increasing the power of the P3's does this: Precise, Present tense and Positive as you plan your action steps.

Where most people go wrong is to make a huge commitment without breaking it up into powerful action steps. We've spoken before about using the Five Percent principle (improve yourself just five percent today) and the Replacement Theory (instead of trying to change a bad habit — replace it with a positive one). These concepts are critical to long-term sustainable change.

Instead of saying, "I'm not going to be so lazy..."

Say, "Today, I will walk ten minutes, two times. Once before lunch and once before I drive home from work."

Each time you accomplish that checkpoint, mark it off. Every time you mark it off, it will boost your confidence and motivate you to do even more.

A CHECKPOINT MAP

A fun way to create your checkpoints is to use post-it notes on a poster size piece of paper. It is a very visual and engaging way to make a map of your checkpoints.

Once you have completed your Checkpoint Map, you can transfer your Action Steps to a daily or weekly planner. Think of this as intentionally making an appointment with your future.

Many people lead lives responding to the needs or emergencies of others. Influential people are the opposite. They know how they want to grow, whom they need to see and make a personal plan of pursuing those commitments.

An additional key to growing exponentially is to plan your favorite activities during times that might be "danger points" for you. For example, if you know that you have a problem with drinking on Friday nights, plan to have dinner or work out with a sober friend. Plan that event when you would normally start drinking.

This is another example of "Replacement Theory," replace a negative behavior with a positive one. Whatever you do, don't wait for the incident to occur and then try to respond in the moment. Prevent the incident by planning ahead.

Recovery counselors often call this Behavioral Mapping. Mapping the locations where we are most likely to have problems.

Recovery counselors often call this Behavioral Mapping. Mapping the locations where we are most likely to have problems. We know ahead of time the places, people and circumstances — the where, who and when — we are most prone to have to make suboptimal decisions. The key is planning to be some place else, with someone else or create a strategy to do something else at those critical junctures.

Take time now to begin securing your future. Write out your action steps today.

See Activity 4.4: Your Checkpoint Map

Activity 4.1: Commitment Discussions

Talk to 3 people you admire about commitments they have made or long-term goals they pursued. Ask them what commitments they think would be positive in your life.

COMMITMENT HALL OF FAME

Name of Person	Committments
My Brother	**Their Commitments** *His commitment to his faith, family and fitness have helped him stay strong in his race against cancer.*
	Suggestions to you *My brother encourages me to put relationships first and to block off time to myself.*

Name of Person	Committments
	Their Commitments
	Suggestions to you

Name of Person	Committments
	Their Commitments
	Suggestions to you

Activity 4.2:
Make a Commitment to Yourself

Write down the 7 Areas of Balance.

Begin by choosing just one area of balance where you would like to focus your growth this week.

Create a statement in that area using the 3P's, personal, positive and present tense.

Add at least three "Checkpoints" that will indicate you are moving closer to your commitment this week. Checkpoints further describe your commitment, they are indications (signs) you are moving towards your goal.

Start small (5 percent) and build. As you feel confidence growing in one area, add additional commitments. At this point you should be feeling an increasing sense of influence in your life. You are focusing on what you can do and what you do have. Your competence will deepen as you exert more personal direction over your life.

Commitment Checkpoint Guide (Sample)

Steps to Excellence

1. Choose the area of balance you would like to focus your growth this week.

2. Create a Commitment Statement (using the 3P's) is motivates you to grow in that particular area.

3. Add at least three checkpoints indicating how you can move closer to that Commitment this week. Checkpoints further define your commitments moving you closer to your goals.

COMMITMENT AREA
Relational

COMMITMENT STATEMENT
"I am a positive and compassionate person who motivates others to reach their fullest potential."

CHECKPOINT 1:
When I laugh, it is with people, not at people.

CHECKPOINT 2:
Sincere people surround me. People who empathize with others and are active in causes that inspire them.

CHECKPOINT 3:
People find me inspiring and feel more hopeful as a result of the time they spend with me.

Commitment Checkpoint Guide (Your Turn)

COMMITMENT AREA

COMMITMENT STATEMENT

CHECKPOINT 1:

CHECKPOINT 2:

CHECKPOINT 3:

Print out this form and repeat it for the other areas of your life when you are ready to start developing them. Remember, start with five percent and work your way up. You have a lifetime to grow your commitments so don't feel like you have to do it all at once.

Activity 4.3:
Strike Out the Cop-Out Words

From Cop Outs to Stand Ups: Stand up for who you are becoming, use words that back up your commitments.

Sample Cop Outs	Sample Stand Outs
"I'll try..."	*"I will..."*
"I can't..."	*"I choose not to at this time."*
"Someday I'll..."	*"On this date, I will..."*
"Maybe I'll..."	*"You can count on me to..."*

Personal Cop Outs	Personal Stand Outs

Activity 4.4: A Checkpoint Map

Begin by writing your commitment on a post-it note on the left side of the paper. At the top of the paper write "Why," on the left side and "What," on the right side. This will remind you that when you read your map to the right, you are reading what you need to do and when you read the map to the left, you will be reading why you need to do it.

To the right of your commitment statement, begin putting up post-it notes explaining what you need to do in order to reach your commitment. As you progress, keep your map simple using the following guidelines:

1. Keep your notes as short as possible, preferably two words, an action verb and a defining noun. For example, "Eat carrots."

2. Later, when you've completed your Checkpoint Map, go back and assign dates and times to each post-it note, "When will I complete this action step?"

Once completed, you should be able to look at your Checkpoint Map and immediately know WHY you will do WHAT you will do and WHEN you will do it.

(See following page for sample)

Checkpoint Map for Your Compassionate Life

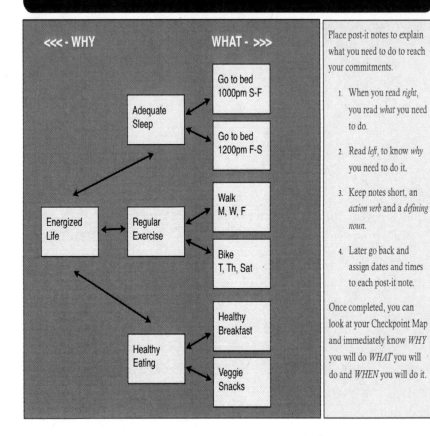

<<< - WHY

WHAT - >>>

Adequate Sleep

Go to bed 1000pm S-F

Go to bed 1200pm F-S

Energized Life

Regular Exercise

Walk M, W, F

Bike T, Th, Sat

Healthy Eating

Healthy Breakfast

Veggie Snacks

Place post-it notes to explain what you need to do to reach your commitments.

1. When you read *right*, you read *what* you need to do.

2. Read *left*, to know *why* you need to do it.

3. Keep notes short, an *action verb* and a *defining noun*.

4. Later go back and assign dates and times to each post-it note.

Once completed, you can look at your Checkpoint Map and immediately know *WHY* you will do *WHAT* you will do and *WHEN* you will do it.

V
Network

Your Proactive Vision Network

Strap On Your Jet Pack — It's Time for Takeoff

Let's begin this chapter by reviewing two important statements we've made throughout this guidebook.

1. "Influence is the ability to build a network of support around your compassionate focus."

2. "The more influential you are, the more you spend your week planning WHO you are going to motivate, not WHAT you are going to do."

So far, you've worked diligently to compile a values statement, articulate your compassionate focus and develop commitments and action steps around that focus. That was your fuselage and wings, now it is time to add a jet pack to your flying machine.

We examined the concept of "Six

Networking Strategy

1. "Influence is the ability to build a network of support around your compassionate focus."

2. "The more influential you are, the more you spend your week planning WHO you are going to motivate, not WHAT you are going to do."

Degrees of Separation," and "Six Pixels of Separation." The research behind these concepts is impressive. For example, in 1967, Social Psychologist Stanley Milgram asked 167 students in Nebraska to connect with a stockbroker in Boston. This stockbroker was unknown to the students, but the students were instructed to pass letters to anyone they believed might be "socially closer to the target." Every letter was delivered and the average number of links — to deliver the letters — was six.

Thirty-six years later, Duncan Watts — a physicist at Columbia University — decided to repeat the experiment, this time using the Internet as part of his work. He recruited 61,000 people worldwide, requesting they send letters to one of 18 targets.

Once again the concept held true. Both the six degrees and the six pixels theory were verified. Just as with Dr. Milgram's study — Professor Watts study found the average number of connections was six links.

Put It To The Test

I've constantly put this theory to the test on a personal and professional basis to expand my own network and the network of others (as in the story of Luis Rodriquez and Juan).

One class I was teaching with high school students was about the power of forgiveness. Students went online to find symbols of forgiveness and some came across a powerful video by award-winning, Canadian songwriter, Peter Katz.

His song, Forgiveness, was written to honor Christopher Berg, whose son, Nicholas, was abducted by terrorists in 2004 while reporting on the war in Iraq. The terrorists held Nicholas for a short time and then beheaded him. US Forces found the terrorist cell's leader, Abu Musab al-Zarqawi, and killed him in a bomb attack. When the press picked up the story, they asked the senior Berg, if he felt justice had been served.

Christopher's response surprised the world. He said he had already forgiven al-Zarqawi and he believed bloodshed only led to more bloodshed. While some admired Mr. Berg's ideals, others disdained him for them. He received numerous death threats because of his beliefs.

When my students heard the story behind Peter's song and saw the video, they wanted to share it with others. We put together a letter to Peter to ask his permission to use the song in our class.

To our surprise and delight, Peter not only sent an inspirational letter about the song, but also stated he would be willing to support our students in other ways if possible. We exchanged a few more e-mails and were stunned when Peter offered to come and do a fund-raising concert for our students and to visit our classrooms as well.

Since then, Peter has been a regular visitor to many of the Outreach Centres and schools where I work across Canada. He always has an inspirational message and great advice for the students with whom he shares his story and music. Peter has time for every student and treats each question with grace and dignity.

You can listen to and see Peter live at his web site: *www.peterkatz.com*

THANK YOU, PETER KATZ!

Dream big. Think about the people who inspire you even if they seem outside your reach — especially if they seem outside your reach. The people you want in your support network should be people who have mastered the aspects you articulated in your Compassionate Focus. One thing is sure, if you aim high you just might lasso a star, but if you aim low you will always tie up your own two feet.

A Proactive Network

In building your network of supporters, there is one word you should keep in mind, "Proactive." It is a great word with three meanings:

1. Pro means "forward thinking."

2. Pro also means "positive attitude."

3. Active means not only do these people think positively and into the future, they also think pragmatically — meaning they take action on your behalf. They are movers and shakers. People go to them and gather around them precisely because they are proactive.

These proactive people are the types of people with whom you want to network. They combine two unique qualities you must grow if you are going to be an influential person. They not only *think* creatively, but they have the unique ability to *apply* their creative thoughts to practical applications.

Innovators not only *think* creatively, but they have the unique ability to *apply* their creative thoughts to practical applications.

THOMAS EDISON

Perhaps the most prolific entrepreneur in North American history was inventor and businessman, Thomas Alva Edison (1847 – 1931). His inventions included the phonograph, the motion picture camera and a light bulb that could be used in businesses and homes. In all, Edison held 1,093 patents, not bad for someone who only had three months of schooling, leaving because his teacher said he was "addled." Young Edison couldn't focus in class and his mind often wandered.

Edison speaks about one of his greatest supporters during that time; "My mother was the making of me. She was so true, so sure of me; and I felt I had something to live for, someone I must not disappoint."

After he left school school, Edison's mother, Nancy, took his education into her own hands and wouldn't give up on the young Thomas.

Raised in poverty, Edison set to work early. He sold candy and newspapers on the train route from Port Huron to Detroit. Eventually, he won the exclusive right to sell papers on that line and then published his own newspaper, The Grand Trunk Herald.

When not selling newspapers, Edison was able to convert a railroad car into his first laboratory. This was just the beginning for the young entrepreneur who went on to found fourteen companies including General Electric, still one of the largest publicly traded companies today.

Edison was not the first *inventor* of the light bulb. He was the first one to make it *affordable*. Other inventors created light bulbs but they would burn out too quickly or cost too much for business or home application. It was Edison's commitment to applying his creativity to practical purposes that made him so well known. That... and his persistence.

It is said that it took 10,000 attempts for him to create the first practical light bulb. When asked by a reporter, how he could sustain failure so many times, Edison responded with one of his most famous quotes, "I have not failed. I've just found 10,000 ways that won't work."

"I have not failed. I've just found 10,000 ways that won't work."

Edison will always remain an example of a proactive entrepreneur, applying his creativity and knowledge into practical applications for businesses and homes.

Two major components must become a part of your character if you are to become influential in life:

1. Become Proactive: Apply your creativity to practical uses.

2. Seek out Proactive Mentors: People who are already proactive — master mentors in areas you are determined to grow — coaches who will help you think proactively as well.

Speaking about influential people, make time to learn about Nicholas Cristakis. Time Magazine named him one of the 100 most influential people in the world in 2009 and he was also named one of Foreign Policy Magazine's 100 top global thinkers. Cristakis is a bestselling author and, with James Fowler, wrote the book, *Connected; The Surprising Power of Our Social Networks and How They Shape Our Lives*. In addition to speaking internationally, Dr. Cristakis is Professor of Medicine, Health Care Policy and Sociology at Harvard University.

Professor Cristakis focuses on networks and social capital. He lectures on the importance of connecting with the right people in pursuing goals in your life. Here is a quote from his Ted Talks seminar on the role of networks and obesity:

"If your friends are obese, your risk of obesity is 45 percent higher. ... If your friend's friends are obese, your risk of obesity is 25 percent higher. ... If your friend's friend's friend, someone you probably don't even know, is obese, your risk of obesity is 10 percent higher. It's only when you get to your friend's friend's friend's friends that there's no longer a relationship between that person's body size and your own body size."

The power of networking is just as formidable for positive characteristics like fitness and well-being. The effect is so pervasive that it can be attached to a huge variety of negative and proactive traits from poverty, crime and homelessness to success, leadership and happiness.

Based on his research, networking and social capital may well be the most important factor in becoming influential, more important than wealth, education and intelligence. Choose your networks wisely! No matter where you *start out,* the depth of your social networks will be largely indicative of where you *wind up* in life.

Your Compelling Statement

"What Makes Me Compelling?"

As you are identifying people to broaden your network, there are some very important questions to keep in mind. The first and foremost is, "Why would this person want to become pro-actively involved with me?'

Or, to put it more directly, "What makes me compelling?"

Very few people spend enough time asking that question and yet it is so critical to a meaningful life. We are each born with dignity, but it is our responsibility to make ourselves compelling.

In Chapter 1, we spoke of the 4E's of a Compelling Life.

1. Enchant = en Cantos (latin) to sing

Put a smile on someone's face or a song in someone's heart.

2. Enthuse = en Theos (Greek) God's fire

An in-burning fire that ignites those around you.

3. Engage = en Gager (French) make a commitment

Make a commitment to something or take a stand.

4. Encourage = en Couer (French) heart

Use COURtesy to put COURage in someone's heart.

Compelling people practice these 4E's until they become habitual. They are radiant people and others are intrinsically drawn to their presence.

It is important here to make a distinction between being a compelling person and having an extroverted or introverted personality. You don't have to be extroverted to be compelling. Some of the most compelling people in the world were also introverted. You can be very reflective and draw people towards you, just as you can be very loud and push people away.

To be compelling means people are drawn to the depth of your compassionate focus and how you have articulated it.

All the work you've put in to creating your values statement and your compassionate focus will now come to fruition. You've done an impressive amount of work to make yourself compelling, now you need to be able to articulate these factors to others in a way that speaks to their hopes and needs — not just *yours*.

When you are connecting with someone you hope to "compel," it is important to understand what engages that person. Work at understanding *their* compassionate focus.

See Activity 5.1

Put It All Together

Consider this powerful quote by US President, Theodore Roosevelt,

> "It is not the critic who counts; not the man who points out how the strong man stumbles, or where the doer of deeds could have done better. The credit belongs to the man who is actually in the arena, who face is marred by dust and sweat and blood, who strives valiantly; who errs and comes short again and again; because there is not effort without error and shortcomings; but who does actually strive to do the deed; who know the great enthusiasm, the great devotion, who spends himself in a worthy cause, who at the best knows in the end the triumph of high achievement and who at the worst, if he fails, at least he fails while daring greatly. So that his place shall never

be with those cold and timid souls who know neither victory nor defeat."

> — Theodore Roosevelt, American,
> 26th US President, 1858-1919)

You have done an incredible amount of work to reach this point. Identifying your values, articulating your Compassionate Focus, creating the tools for a positive social profile, making solid commitments and now identifying the people who can help you make your life soar. Only two things remain.

1. Commit your next steps to writing on a calendar, planner or agenda.

2. Take the necessary action.

We've already learned that making a written commitment to yourself substantially increases the chances you will accomplish that task. You've learned that in order for an action to be effective you must be able to identify *when* you're going to do *what* you're going to do. You know if you plan these important tasks during your "Danger Times" — times when you normally are in the wrong place with the wrong person — you increase the possibilities that you can replace undermining, addictive or compulsive behaviors.

What is left now is to actually act on what you've planned.

You can increase the odds you will take action if you share your plan with someone who values you. Ask them to follow-up on a regular basis to find out how things worked.

You will need four items to make your initial contact.

1. The Compassionate Focus you made for the person with whom you are connecting.

2. The Networking Tree you created to reach that person.

3. Your Compelling Invitation (and a shortened version with contact information just in case you can't directly reach the person with whom you are networking and talk to their assistant instead).

4. The questions you are going to ask the individual and the action step you are requesting they make.

See Activity 5.2, Build a Networking Tree

Meeting With Your Destiny

My friends, the universe welcomes the bold and wise, but in a balanced combination. Boldness without wisdom is arrogance. Wisdom without boldness is self-deception. Act on what you believe and your life will be full of meaning.

Boldness without wisdom is arrogance. Wisdom without boldness is self-deception.

Now is your opportunity to be compelling; enCHANT, enTHUSE, enCOURAGE, enGAGE!

Don't let the momentum of the moment fade. To have a lasting impact, make the first commitment of each week be a commitment to yourself. Set aside the time to plan out your week by your Compassionate Focus. Put that time into your calendar regularly. Make it a habit.

Here are the specific questions to ask during the "meeting with your destiny."

1. Has my Values Statement deepened in any way? Do I still believe in my Values Statement — "No matter what?"

2. Has my Compassionate Focus evolved in any way? Are there new things that have occurred or people I have met that enhanced my focus?

3. How am I progressing relative to my Commitment Check Points? Do I need to update any of them?

4. What are the primary Action Steps I need to take this week to further my Commitments? When will I take them?

5. Are there any "Danger Areas," this week I need to replace with positive actions, people or places?

6. With whom do I need to network this week? What is my plan for connecting with them? When am I going to take that action?

Destiny is an interesting word. Some people would call it your fate — but you know better than that.

Your destiny is the sum total of the choices you make, the actions you take, challenges you utilize, commitments you live by and the people with whom you decide to associate.

Working through this guidebook was a huge step towards mastering your own destiny. I hope you will feel free to keep me informed as to how your Compassionate Life unfolds.

"Watch your thoughts, for they become words. Watch your words, for they become actions. Watch your actions, for they become habits. Watch your habits, for they become character. Watch your character, for it becomes destiny."

— Anonymous

"Watch your thoughts, for they become words. Watch your words, for they become actions. Watch your actions, for they become habits. Watch your habits, for they become character. Watch your character, for it becomes destiny." — Anonymous

See Activity 5.3 Purpose-Full Planner

Inspiring Quotes by Influential People

ABRAHAM LINCOLN

"The best way to destroy an enemy is to make him a friend."
Abraham Lincoln (American 16th US President (1861-65)

WILL ROGERS

"I never met a man I didn't like." Will Rogers (American entertainer and social commentator, 1879-1935)

Rogers was part Cherokee and quipped that his ancestors didn't come over on the Mayflower but they "met the boat."

THOMAS EDISON

"Genius is one percent inspiration, ninety-nine percent perspiration."

"I have not failed. I've just found 10,000 ways that won't work."

"Many of life's failures are men who did not realize how close they were to success when they gave up."

"Nearly every man who develops an idea works at it up to the point where it looks impossible, and then gets discouraged. That's not the place to become discouraged."

"Opportunity is missed by most people because it is dressed in overalls and looks like work."

RANDOM QUOTES

"If you only do what you know you can do — you never do very much." Tom Krause (Speaker, teacher and coach, b.1934)

"Take time to deliberate; but when the time for action arrives, stop thinking and go in." Andrew Jackson (American, 7th US President, 1767-1845)

"Whatever course you decide upon, there is always someone to tell you that you are wrong. There are always difficulties arising which tempt you to believe that your critics are right. To map out a course of action and follow it to an end requires courage." Ralph Waldo Emerson (American poet, lecturer, essayist, 1803-1882)

"I've learned that people will forget what you said, people will forget what you did, but people will never forget how you made them feel." Maya Angelou (American poet, b.1928)

Activity 5.1:
Networking Preparation Form

Name the person you want to invite into your network

Research that person on the web or through others who might know him or her

Fill in the four areas of their compassionate focus as best you can.

1. What causes move them? Who inspires them?

2. What personality strengths make them unique? Do you think they are predominantly relational, strategic, outgoing or prone to action?

3. What talents or gifts have they mastered?

4. Who is in their network?

Now that you've done that homework, it is time for you to take the next step. Complete the next two questions:

1. What do I hope to learn from this person?

2. What action am I asking them to consider?

That second question is really important to examine. You're not just asking for an autograph or planning a pleasant visit. A well-considered request will honor the person with whom you are talking. To have no request — or a poorly matched request — is likely to leave that person questioning your sincerity.

There are three last items to remember before you consider contacting someone.

1. First, close by asking this question: "Is there something that — because of my inexperience — I missed asking but you would be willing to share with me?"

2. Secondly, ask the person you are with if they have other people with whom you should network. If that person has found you compelling they might even offer to introduce you. The best way to grow your network is by fostering word-of-mouth. Help people speak on your behalf.

3. Finally, always, ALWAYS, and in ALL WAYS say, "Thank you."

Take time to send a personal card giving a specific compliment to the individual who offered time to you. Time and relationship are an influential person's most valued commodities — far more than important than possessions or positions.

Hand-written cards are so rare these days and so, deeply appreciated when they are received. It will tell the person you've just met that you are thoughtful and have class.

Send a thank you note regardless of the outcome of your interaction. Keep in mind it is a good thing when someone challenges your comfort zone or beliefs. People who tell you the truth — even when it hurts — are proactive too. See their comments as a challenge not as negative. There is rarely growth in 1) maintaining the status quo, 2) being indifferent or 3) hanging around people who only tell you what you want to hear. Such behavior deceptively undermines your growth.

PREPARING TO NETWORK

Step 1

Name of Person: _____ ACT WITH CONVICTION

What is his/her unique
personality strengths?

What moves him/her?
Who inspires him/her?

What does
he / she
value?

What skills or talents does
he/she want to master?

Who supports his/her
compassionate focus?

Step 2

Prepare, then act with conviction

The following questions will help you refine your compelling invitation. Once completed, find someone to help you practice your invitation.

Overview Questions

1. What do I hope to learn from this person?

_____

_____

2. What action am I asking them to consider?

_____

_____

Specific Questions

1. Do I know anyone networked to this person who can introduce or refer him/her to me?

_____

_____

2. What is the best way to introduce myself to him/her?

_____

_____

3. Who can help me work on a compelling invitation, allow me to practice my introduction and role-play a discussion with this person?

_____

_____

You are ready to ACT! Keep your momentum going. One of the greatest mantras for influence is, "Do it NOW!"

Activity 5.2 Build a Networking Tree

WHO TO HOW

Now we're going to build another tree similar to your Action Step Tree from Chapter 4. The previous tree focused on Why to What. When you read the chart to the right, you read what you were going to do. When you read the chart to the left, you read why you were going to do it. A "What (task)" without a Why (meaning)" become mundane. It is when we know the purpose behind our actions that we are fully energized.

A Networking Tree reads from Who to How. The left side will indicate whom you want to reach and as you follow it to the right you will examine how to reach them.

Just like with the Action Step tree, you can create this tree on a poster board with post-it notes. Once you have completed the chart, go back and assign when you will do what. Examine the sample chart and use it as an example for meeting some-one you would like to know but might find distant — or even impossible — to reach.

Remember, you are not looking for a celebrity's autograph here. You are seeking to create a proactive relationship with someone who is a master in your area of interest.

Your Network Tree (Sample)

Goal: *Ask Hannah Taylor of the Ladybug Foundation to speak to our community about homelessness.*

Who > How

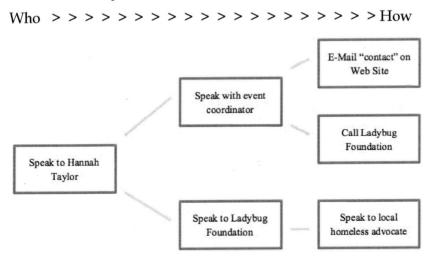

Your Network Tree

Goal: Exercise

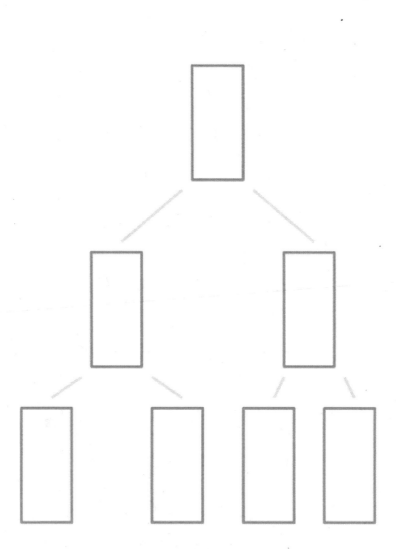

Who ＞＞＞＞＞＞＞＞＞＞＞＞＞＞＞＞＞＞＞＞ How

5.3: Your Purpose-Full Planner

PURPOSE-FULL PLANNER

My Values Statement

Has my Values Statement deepened? If so, how?

Has my Compassionate Focus evolved? If so, how?

Am I getting closer to achieving my Checkpoints (review them and make any necessary changes)?

What Action Steps are my priorities this week and when will I do them?

1. _____

2. _____

3. _____

Are there any danger moments that I need to replace with positive people, actions or places?

1. _____

2. _____

3. _____

Who do I need to network with this week and how will I connect with them?

1. _____

2. _____

3. _____

Use this area to write a weekly Inspiring Quote.

Monday
Time: _____
Task: _____
Time: _____
Task: _____
Time: _____
Task: _____

Tuesday
Time: _____
Task: _____
Time: _____
Task: _____
Time: _____
Task: _____

Wednesday
Time: _____
Task: _____
Time: _____
Task: _____
Time: _____
Task: _____

Thursday
Time: _____
Task: _____
Time: _____
Task: _____
Time: _____
Task: _____

Friday
Time: _____
Task: _____
Time: _____
Task: _____
Time: _____
Task: _____

Saturday / Sunday
Time: _____
Task: _____
Time: _____
Task: _____
Time: _____
Task: _____

Bibliography

Bradberry, Travis and Greaves, Jean. (2009). Emotional Intelligence, 2.0. Talent Smart

Cristokis, MD, PhD., Nicolas A, and Folwer, PhD, James H. (2009) Connected; The surprising power of social networkds and how they shape our lives. Little, Brown and Company, New York

Gardner, Howard. (2006). Five Minds for the Future. Harvard Business School Press

Goleman, Daniel. (1998). Emotional Intelligence. Bantam Books

Goleman, Daniel. (2005). Social Intelligence; The New Science of Human Relationships. Bantam Books

Joel, Mitch. (2012) Six Pixels of Separation; Everyone's Connected. Grand Central Publishing

Milgram, Stanley. (1967). The Small World Problem. Psychology Today. Vol. 2: 60 – 67

Rath, Tom. (2007). Strengthfinders 2.0. Gallup Press

Rodriquez, Luis J. (1995). Always Running: La Vida Loca; Gang Days in L.A. Scholarly Books

Pink, Daniel. (2005). A Whole New Mind. Penguin Books

Watts, D.J.; Strogratz, S.H. (1998). Collective dynamis of "Small-world netorks." Nature, 393 (6684): 440 – 442

Zak, Paul. (2008). Moral Markets: The Critical Role of Values in the Economy. Princeton University Press